Social Media Success

Proven Strategies to Build a Following and Drive Sales Using Psychology

By James Landry

Table of Contents

Chapter 6: Building Community and Fostering Engagement

Creating a Sense of Belonging

Engaging with Your Audience

Collaborations with Other Profiles

Chapter 7: Maximizing Your Reach

Understanding Social Media Algorithms

Importance of Early Interaction

Platform-Specific Insights

Danger of Reposting the Same Content

Chapter 8: The Power of Blogging for Social Media and SEO

Boosting Social Media Presence with Blogs

Improving Google Rankings

Combining Blogs with Social Media

Chapter 9: Sharing Knowledge to Build Trust

Value of Sharing Information

Creating Educational Content

Chapter 10: Analyzing and Adapting Your Strategy

Monitoring Performance

Adapting Based on Feedback

Avoiding Overreaction

Chapter 11: Overcoming Challenges
Dealing with Negative Feedback
Avoiding Burnout

Chapter 12: Case Studies and Success Stories
Learning from the Best

Chapter 13: Future Trends in Social Media
Emerging Platforms and Technologies
Staying Ahead of the Curve

Conclusion

Appendix

Introduction

Overview of Social Media's Influence

Social media has become an integral part of modern communication, permeating every aspect of our daily lives. From personal interactions to professional networking, social media platforms have revolutionized the way we connect, share information, and engage with the world. The pervasive role of social media in modern communication cannot be overstated. Platforms like Facebook, Instagram, Twitter, TikTok, and LinkedIn have created a global village where information can be shared instantly and widely. These platforms have made it possible for individuals to maintain relationships across great distances and for businesses to reach audiences worldwide with unprecedented ease.

The rise of social media has blurred the lines between personal and professional lives. Professionals now use platforms like LinkedIn to build networks and advance their careers, while businesses leverage Instagram and Facebook to create brand identities and engage with customers. Social media has also democratized content creation, allowing anyone with a smartphone to become a content creator and influencer. This shift has fundamentally changed how we interact with each other and how we consume information.

In an era where authenticity is highly valued, building a genuine social media presence is crucial. Authenticity fosters trust and loyalty, encouraging followers to engage more deeply with your content. A strong social media presence not only enhances personal and professional relationships but also establishes credibility and authority in your field. This credibility is essential for converting casual followers into dedicated fans or customers. By being authentic, you create a more relatable and trustworthy image, which can significantly impact your social media success.

One of the significant advantages of building a social media following is the ability to connect with your target audience without the need for expensive advertising campaigns. Unlike traditional advertising methods that require significant financial investment, social media allows you to reach your target audience organically. By creating engaging and valuable content, you can attract followers who are genuinely interested in what you have to offer, leading to higher engagement rates and better conversion rates. Additionally, social media platforms offer detailed analytics and insights, enabling you to refine your strategies and improve your results over time.

While email lists have been a staple of digital marketing for years, social media offers unique advantages. Studies have shown that social media can be more effective than email lists in terms of engagement and reach. According to recent research, social media platforms like Facebook and Instagram have higher engagement rates compared to email campaigns. This is because social media allows for more interactive and visually appealing content, making it easier to capture and retain the audience's attention.

Purpose of the Book

The primary aim of this book is to provide you with a comprehensive understanding of the psychological principles that drive social media engagement. By demystifying these principles, the book aims to equip you with actionable strategies to build and maintain a dedicated following. Understanding the psychological factors that influence user behavior on social media is essential for creating content that resonates with your audience. This book will explore various cognitive biases, emotional triggers, and social dynamics that drive engagement, providing you with a solid foundation to build your social media strategy.

Beyond theory, this book offers practical advice and proven techniques to help you attract and retain followers. From creating compelling content to leveraging social media algorithms, you'll learn how to implement strategies that drive real results. Each chapter is designed to provide you with actionable steps that you can apply immediately to your social media efforts. Whether you're just starting out or looking to refine your existing strategy, this book will provide valuable insights and guidance.

Content is king in the world of social media. This book will guide you through the process of creating content that not only captures attention but also fosters long-term engagement. You'll learn how to craft stories, visuals, and messages that resonate deeply with your audience, turning followers into loyal fans. By understanding what makes content compelling and how to create it, you'll be able to build a strong and engaged following that will support your goals.

The Pitfalls of Purchasing Fake Followers and Likes

In the quest to build a social media following, some individuals and businesses resort to purchasing fake followers and likes. While this might seem like a quick fix, it can have detrimental effects on your credibility and overall social media strategy. Fake followers and likes are easily detectable and can severely damage your reputation. Authenticity and trust are paramount on social media, and when your audience discovers that you've inflated your follower count artificially, it can lead to a loss of credibility and trust.

Social media algorithms prioritize content based on engagement metrics such as likes, comments, and shares. Fake followers and likes do not engage genuinely with your content, leading to lower overall engagement rates. This can negatively affect your content's visibility and ranking on social media platforms. The algorithms are designed to promote content that generates genuine engagement, so fake followers can actually hinder your efforts to reach a wider audience.

There have been numerous instances where social media platforms have penalized accounts for purchasing fake followers. These penalties can include reduced visibility, suspension, or even permanent banning of the account. Highlighting these real-world examples underscores the risks associated with such practices. It's important to build your following organically and focus on genuine engagement rather than taking shortcuts that can backfire.

Building a genuine following takes time and effort, but it is far more rewarding in the long run. Authentic followers are more likely to engage with your content, share it with others, and convert into customers or clients. A genuine following also provides valuable feedback and insights, helping you refine your content and strategies for better results. By focusing on organic growth, you can build a strong and engaged community that will support your brand and help you achieve your goals.

Words of Wisdom: Finding Your Unique Path

As you embark on this journey to build a successful social media presence, it's important to remember that there is no one-size-fits-all approach. The strategies and principles outlined in this book can be applied to various types of content, whether it's videos of you speaking, still images, or any other creative format you come up with. However, it's crucial to choose a path that fits you, the person posting. Authenticity and comfort are key. If you're not comfortable with a particular style or approach, it will likely show in your content, and your audience will sense it.

Don't feel pressured to mimic what others are doing just because it works for them. What works for someone else might not work for you, and that's okay. Social media success comes from finding your unique voice and style, and connecting with your audience in a way that feels natural and genuine to you. The principles in this book are designed to help you navigate this journey and find the approach that works best for you.

Remember, the goal is to build a genuine and engaged following that resonates with your content. By applying the psychological principles and strategies discussed in this book, you can create content that not only attracts followers but also fosters deep and meaningful connections with them. This will ultimately lead to a more successful and fulfilling social media presence.

Chapter 1: The Basics of Social Media Psychology

Understanding the psychology behind social media is essential for creating content that truly resonates with your audience. In this chapter, we'll explore the fundamental psychological principles that drive social media engagement, giving you the knowledge you need to develop a more effective social media strategy.

Understanding Human Behavior Online

Social media platforms are designed to capture and hold our attention. They do this by tapping into fundamental aspects of human psychology. To create content that resonates, it's crucial to understand these psychological principles.

Cognitive Biases and Their Impact on Social Media Behavior

Cognitive biases are systematic patterns of deviation from norm or rationality in judgment. These biases affect how we perceive and interact with information online. On social media, cognitive biases play a significant role in how users engage with content. One key bias is *confirmation bias*, which refers to our tendency to search for, interpret, and remember information in a way that confirms our preconceptions. On social media, this means users are more likely to engage with content that aligns with their existing beliefs and opinions. Understanding confirmation bias can help you create content that resonates more deeply with your audience by aligning with their views or challenging them in a way that feels constructive.

Another important bias is *social proof*, the psychological phenomenon where people assume the actions of others in an attempt to reflect correct behavior. On social media, this is often seen in the form of likes, shares, and comments. High engagement on a post signals to others that the content is valuable and trustworthy, encouraging further engagement. Leveraging social proof can amplify the reach and impact of your content. Similarly, the *bandwagon effect* occurs when people do something primarily because others are doing it. This effect can drive viral trends and challenges on social media. Creating content that taps into trending topics or popular movements can help you capitalize on this effect.

The Role of Dopamine in Social Media Usage

Dopamine is a neurotransmitter that plays a key role in the brain's reward system. It's released in response to pleasurable experiences, including social interactions. Social media platforms are designed to trigger dopamine release by providing immediate rewards in the form of likes, comments, and shares. This creates a feedback loop that keeps users coming back for more. When users receive positive feedback on their posts, their brains release dopamine, making them feel good and reinforcing the behavior. This is why notifications and real-time interactions are so addictive. Understanding this mechanism can help you create content that engages your audience and encourages repeat interactions.

The Phenomenon of FOMO (Fear of Missing Out)

FOMO (Fear of Missing Out) is a pervasive anxiety that others might be having rewarding experiences from which one is absent. This fear is amplified by social media, where users are constantly exposed to highlights of others' lives. FOMO drives users to engage with content more frequently and share their own experiences to avoid feeling left out. To leverage FOMO in your content strategy, create exclusive or time-sensitive content that encourages immediate engagement. Limited-time offers, live events, and sneak peeks can all tap into this fear and drive higher engagement.

Follower vs. Following Counts and Their Impact

The ratio of followers to following can significantly affect whether someone decides to follow you. A high follower count with a relatively low following count often signals to users that an account is authoritative, popular, and worth following. This phenomenon is tied to social proof, where people are more likely to follow an account that many others are following. Conversely, accounts that follow many but have few followers may be perceived as less credible. Being mindful of your follower-to-following ratio can help you manage perceptions and attract more followers.

People's Willingness to Comment and Like Based on Others' Actions

The willingness of users to engage with content by commenting or liking is often influenced by the actions of others. When users see that a post has many likes or comments, they are more likely to engage themselves, a concept rooted in social proof and the bandwagon effect. This behavior is particularly evident in the comment sections of posts. A post with many comments creates a sense of community and conversation, encouraging others to join in. This is why initial engagement is so critical; it sets the tone for how future users will interact with your content. Encouraging early engagement through strategic calls-to-action or engaging with early commenters can help build this momentum.

The Impact of Visual Content on Engagement

Visual content is a powerful tool for capturing attention and driving engagement on social media. Humans are highly visual creatures, and our brains process images much faster than text. This makes high-quality images, videos, and graphics essential for standing out in a crowded social media feed. Content with compelling visuals tends to receive more likes, shares, and comments, enhancing its overall reach and impact. Investing in good visual content can significantly boost your social media presence.

The Role of Consistency in Building Trust

Consistency in posting schedules, content themes, and brand voice is crucial for building trust with your audience. When followers know what to expect from your social media accounts, they are more likely to engage regularly. Inconsistent posting or drastic changes in content can confuse and alienate your audience. Establishing a consistent presence helps reinforce your brand identity and keeps your audience engaged over the long term.

The Science of Engagement

Creating engaging content is both an art and a science. By understanding the psychological triggers that drive social media interactions, you can craft content that captures attention and encourages action.

Behavioral Triggers That Drive Social Media Interactions

Understanding what motivates users to interact with content is key to driving engagement. Some common triggers include curiosity, which can draw users in and encourage them to click, like, or share. Use intriguing headlines, questions, and teasers to pique curiosity. Additionally, emotional triggers play a crucial role. Content that evokes strong emotions such as joy, surprise, anger, or sadness tends to be more engaging. People are more likely to share content that makes them feel something deeply.

Visual and emotional stimuli are powerful tools in capturing attention on social media. High-quality images, videos, and graphics can make your content stand out in a crowded feed. Visual content is processed faster by the brain, making it more likely to capture attention quickly. Pairing compelling visuals with emotional storytelling can significantly enhance engagement.

How Social Validation Shapes Online Behavior and Community Dynamics

Social validation, or the desire to seek approval from others, shapes online behavior and community dynamics. On social media, this is evident in the way users seek likes, comments, and shares as a form of validation. Creating content that encourages positive feedback and interaction can build a sense of community and belonging among your followers. Encouraging user-generated content and fostering conversations can enhance this sense of community.

The Importance of Authenticity in Social Media

Authenticity is a critical component of successful social media engagement. Users are drawn to content that feels real and relatable. Sharing personal stories, behind-the-scenes glimpses, and genuine interactions can help build a stronger connection with your audience. Authenticity fosters trust and loyalty, making followers more likely to engage with your content and support your brand.

The Psychological Effects of Negative Social Media Interactions

Negative interactions, such as criticism and trolling, are an inevitable part of social media. Understanding the psychological impact of these interactions is important for managing them effectively. Negative comments can discourage engagement and affect the overall tone of your community. Developing strategies for handling negative feedback, such as responding constructively or moderating comments, can help maintain a positive environment.

By understanding these psychological principles, you can create a more effective social media strategy that not only attracts followers but also engages them deeply. The insights gained from cognitive biases, dopamine responses, FOMO, social proof, follower-to-following ratios, and the bandwagon effect will help you craft content that resonates with your audience on a fundamental level. This knowledge is the foundation upon which successful social media strategies are built, setting the stage for the more detailed tactics and approaches covered in the subsequent chapters.

Chapter 2: Building a Solid Foundation

Before you can create engaging content and build a loyal following, it's essential to establish a strong foundation. This involves choosing the right type of content for each platform and creating a consistent brand identity. By laying a solid groundwork, you'll ensure that your social media efforts are effective and sustainable.

Choosing the Right Type of Content for Each Platform

Each social media platform has its unique characteristics and user base. To maximize your impact, it's crucial to tailor your content to fit the platform you're using.

Overview of Major Social Media Platforms

1. Instagram: Known for its visual-centric content, Instagram is ideal for sharing high-quality photos, videos, and stories. Its user base skews younger, with a strong presence of influencers and brands. Instagram is great for showcasing lifestyle content, behind-the-scenes glimpses, and visual storytelling. Leveraging Instagram Stories and IGTV can enhance engagement by providing diverse content formats. Stories offer a way to share more casual, ephemeral content that can drive immediate interaction, while IGTV allows for longer, more in-depth video content.

2. Facebook: With a diverse user base spanning all age groups, Facebook is a versatile platform for sharing a wide range of content, including text updates, photos, videos, and links. It's particularly effective for building

communities through groups and engaging with followers through comments and messages. Facebook Live is a powerful tool for real-time engagement, allowing you to host live events, Q&A sessions, and interactive discussions.

3. Twitter/X: Twitter is characterized by its fast-paced, real-time nature. It's ideal for sharing short updates, news, and engaging in conversations. The platform's user base is varied, with a strong presence of professionals, influencers, and news organizations. Twitter is excellent for real-time engagement, trending topics, and customer service. Utilizing Twitter Lists can help you organize and follow specific groups or topics, enhancing your ability to engage with niche communities.

4. TikTok: Known for its short, engaging videos, TikTok appeals primarily to a younger audience. The platform thrives on trends, challenges, and creative content.

TikTok is perfect for showcasing personality, humor, and creative expression through video. Using popular sounds and participating in trending challenges can significantly boost your visibility and engagement on TikTok.

5. LinkedIn: Focused on professional networking, LinkedIn is best for sharing industry insights, professional achievements, and thought leadership content. Its user base consists mainly of professionals and businesses, making it an ideal platform for B2B marketing and professional branding. LinkedIn Articles and LinkedIn Live are excellent features for providing in-depth insights and real-time professional engagement.

We will dive into more specific strategies for maximizing your reach and engagement on these platforms in Chapter 7.

Assessing Platform Demographics and Aligning Content Types with Your Target Audience

Understanding the demographics of each platform is essential for tailoring your content effectively. For example, if your target audience is primarily teenagers and young adults, TikTok and Instagram might be the best platforms to focus on. Conversely, if you're targeting professionals and businesses, LinkedIn and Twitter might be more appropriate.

When aligning content types with your target audience, consider their preferences and behaviors. For instance, younger audiences may prefer short, entertaining videos, while professionals might engage more with informative articles and thought leadership posts. Conducting audience research and creating detailed audience personas can help you understand these preferences better. We'll discuss how to conduct audience research and create personas in Chapter 3.

Factors to Consider When Tailoring Content for Each Platform

1. Content Format: Each platform has preferred content formats. Instagram favors high-quality images and short videos, while TikTok thrives on creative, engaging video content. LinkedIn is more suitable for long-form articles and professional updates. Understanding and leveraging the preferred formats can enhance your content's effectiveness and reach.

2. Engagement Style: The way users engage with content varies across platforms. Instagram and Facebook encourage visual engagement through likes and comments, while Twitter focuses on real-time interactions and retweets. Tailor your engagement strategies to fit the platform's unique style. For example, asking open-ended questions in your posts can drive comments and discussions, while sharing timely updates on Twitter can encourage retweets and real-time engagement. We will explore different engagement strategies in Chapter 6.

3. Posting Frequency: The optimal posting frequency differs for each platform. Twitter requires more frequent updates due to its fast-paced nature, while Instagram and Facebook benefit from consistent but less frequent posts. LinkedIn posts can be less frequent but should offer substantial value. Developing a posting schedule that aligns with each platform's dynamics can help maintain audience interest and engagement.

4. Hashtags and Trends: Utilizing platform-specific hashtags and participating in trends can boost your content's visibility. For example, TikTok's trending challenges and Instagram's popular hashtags can help your content reach a wider audience. Researching and using relevant hashtags can increase your content's discoverability and engagement.

5. Algorithm Preferences: Each platform's algorithm favors different types of content and engagement. Understanding these preferences can help you optimize your posts for maximum reach. For instance, Instagram's algorithm prioritizes engagement within the first hour of posting,

while LinkedIn's algorithm rewards content that sparks meaningful interactions. Analyzing and adapting to algorithm changes can enhance your content's performance.

Importance of Businesses, Brands, and Entrepreneurs Being Present on All Platforms

While it's essential to tailor your content to each platform, maintaining a presence across multiple platforms can enhance your overall reach and impact. Each platform offers unique opportunities to connect with different segments of your audience. By diversifying your social media strategy, you can maximize your brand's visibility and engagement.

Being present on multiple platforms also provides a safety net in case one platform experiences issues or changes its algorithms. Diversification ensures that your brand remains visible and accessible to your audience, regardless of platform-specific challenges.

Leveraging Cross-Promotion

Cross-promotion involves using one social media platform to promote your presence on another platform. This strategy can help you grow your audience across multiple platforms by encouraging followers to connect with you in different spaces. For example, you can use Instagram Stories to promote a new YouTube video or tweet about a Facebook live event. Cross-promotion not only increases your visibility but also helps create a cohesive brand experience across different platforms. We'll discuss cross-promotion techniques in more detail in Chapter 7.

Creating a Consistent Brand Identity

A consistent brand identity is crucial for building trust and recognition. It involves maintaining a cohesive visual identity, crafting a compelling bio, and establishing a consistent tone and voice across all your content.

The Importance of a Cohesive Visual Identity

Your visual identity includes elements such as logos, color schemes, fonts, and overall aesthetics. A cohesive visual identity helps create a recognizable brand image that stands out in users' feeds. Consistency in visual elements reinforces your brand's presence and makes your content instantly identifiable.

- Logos and Color Schemes: Use a consistent logo and color palette across all platforms to reinforce your brand identity. This consistency helps create a unified look that users can easily associate with your brand. A well-designed logo and carefully selected color scheme can convey your brand's values and personality, making a lasting impression on your audience.

- Aesthetics and Design: Maintain a consistent aesthetic in your photos, videos, and graphics. Whether you prefer a minimalist design, vibrant colors, or a specific style of photography, consistency in aesthetics builds a strong brand image. Using similar filters, design elements, and visual styles across your content can enhance brand recognition and appeal. We'll explore more about visual content and its impact on engagement in Chapter 3.

Crafting a Compelling and Authentic Bio

Your bio is often the first impression users have of your brand. It's essential to craft a bio that captures your brand essence and communicates your value proposition clearly and authentically.

- Clarity and Conciseness: Keep your bio clear and concise, highlighting what your brand stands for and what users can expect from your content. Use keywords relevant to your niche to improve discoverability. A well-crafted bio should provide a snapshot of your brand's mission, values, and offerings, enticing users to learn more.

- Authenticity: Be genuine and authentic in your bio. Users are drawn to brands that feel real and relatable. Share your story, mission, and values to create a deeper connection with your audience. Authenticity builds trust and fosters a sense of community, encouraging users to engage with your brand. More on building trust through authenticity will be discussed in Chapter 9.

Establishing a Consistent Tone and Voice in Your Content

The tone and voice of your content play a significant role in building familiarity and trust with your audience. Consistency in how you communicate helps create a cohesive brand experience.

- Tone: Decide on a tone that reflects your brand's personality. Whether it's professional, casual, humorous, or inspirational, maintaining a consistent tone helps users relate to your brand. Your tone should align with your brand's values and resonate with your target audience.

- Voice: Your brand voice should be consistent across all content, from social media posts to customer interactions. A consistent voice reinforces your brand identity and makes your communications more recognizable. Developing a brand voice guide can help ensure consistency in how your brand speaks across different channels. We'll cover more on creating a consistent brand voice in Chapter 4.

Building a Content Calendar

A content calendar is an essential tool for maintaining consistency and organization in your social media strategy. It helps you plan and schedule your posts in advance, ensuring that you have a regular posting schedule and cover all relevant topics and themes. A well-maintained content calendar can be a game-changer for your social media strategy, helping you stay organized, consistent, and strategic in your approach.

Planning Ahead

Use a content calendar to map out your posts for the month or quarter. This planning allows you to align your content with key dates, events, and campaigns. By planning ahead, you can ensure that you are prepared for holidays, product launches, and other significant events that are relevant to your audience. This proactive approach helps you avoid last-minute scrambling and ensures that your content is timely and relevant.

Balancing Content Types

Ensure your content calendar includes a mix of content types, such as educational posts, promotional content, user-generated content, and engagement-driven posts. This balance keeps your audience interested and engaged. Diversifying your content types caters to different audience preferences and maintains their interest. For instance, a well-balanced calendar might include a mix of blog posts, infographics, videos, live sessions, and interactive polls.

Tracking Performance

Use your content calendar to track the performance of your posts. Analyze metrics such as engagement rates, reach, and conversions to identify what works best and refine your strategy accordingly. Regularly reviewing your content's performance helps you understand your audience's preferences and improve your content strategy over time. This data-driven approach ensures that your social media efforts are continuously optimized for better results.

Adjusting and Adapting

A content calendar isn't set in stone. Be prepared to adjust and adapt your calendar based on the performance of your posts and any new opportunities that arise. Flexibility is key to responding to real-time events, trends, and audience feedback. If a particular type of content is performing exceptionally well, consider incorporating more of it into your calendar. Conversely, if something isn't resonating with your audience, don't hesitate to pivot.

Collaborating with Your Team

If you have a team working on your social media strategy, a content calendar helps ensure that everyone is on the same page. It facilitates collaboration by clearly outlining what content needs to be created, who is responsible for it, and when it needs to be published. This collaborative approach ensures that your social media strategy is cohesive and well-executed.

Tools for Building a Content Calendar

There are various tools available that can help you build and manage your content calendar effectively. Platforms like Trello, Asana, and CoSchedule offer features that allow you to plan, schedule, and track your social media posts. These tools can help you stay organized and streamline your content planning process. We'll explore some of these tools in more detail in Chapter 9.

Engaging with Your Audience

Building a strong social media presence isn't just about posting content; it's also about engaging with your audience. Responding to comments, messages, and mentions shows that you value your followers and fosters a sense of community.

- Timely Responses: Respond to comments and messages promptly to show that you are attentive and value your audience's input. Engaging in real-time conversations can strengthen your relationship with followers. We'll delve deeper into best practices for audience engagement in Chapter 6.

- Interactive Content: Use polls, Q&A sessions, and live videos to interact with your audience directly. These interactive formats encourage participation and make your followers feel more connected to your brand.

- User-Generated Content: Encourage your followers to create and share content related to your brand. User-generated content not only provides social proof but also builds a sense of community and belonging.

By building a solid foundation through tailored content, a consistent brand identity, strategic cross-promotion, and active audience engagement, you'll be well-positioned to create engaging and impactful social media content. The next chapters will delve deeper into specific strategies for creating captivating content, leveraging psychological principles, and maximizing your reach.

Chapter 3: Content That Captivates

Creating content that captures attention and engages your audience is the heart of a successful social media strategy. This chapter will explore the essential elements of understanding your audience and crafting content that not only attracts but also retains and captivates your followers.

Understanding Your Audience

Knowing your audience is the first step in creating content that resonates with them. Understanding their preferences, behaviors, and pain points allows you to tailor your content to meet their needs and interests.

Conducting Audience Research

Audience research involves gathering information about your target audience to understand their demographics, interests, and behaviors. This research can be conducted through various methods, such as surveys, interviews, and social media analytics.

- Surveys and Polls: Use surveys and polls to gather direct feedback from your audience. These tools can provide insights into their preferences, interests, and pain points. Platforms like SurveyMonkey or Google Forms can help you create and distribute surveys easily.

- Interviews and Focus Groups: Conducting interviews or focus groups with a small segment of your audience can provide deeper insights into their motivations and behaviors. These qualitative methods allow for more detailed responses and a better understanding of your audience's needs.

- Social Media Analytics: Utilize the analytics tools provided by social media platforms to gain insights into your audience's demographics, engagement patterns, and content preferences. Tools like Facebook Insights, Instagram Analytics, and Twitter Analytics offer valuable data that can help you refine your content strategy. We will explore more on using analytics in Chapter 9.

Creating Detailed Audience Personas

Audience personas are fictional representations of your ideal followers based on the data you gather. These personas help you visualize and understand your audience better, allowing you to create more targeted and effective content.

-   Demographics: Define the basic demographics of your personas, such as age, gender, location, and occupation. This information helps you understand who your audience is and what their general characteristics are.

- Interests and Behaviors: Identify the interests, hobbies, and behaviors of your personas. Understanding what they enjoy and how they spend their time can help you create content that aligns with their interests.

- Pain Points and Needs: Determine the pain points and needs of your personas. What challenges do they face? What problems are they looking to solve? Addressing these issues in your content can make it more relevant and valuable to your audience.

- Content Preferences: Identify the types of content your personas prefer. Do they engage more with videos, articles, infographics, or interactive content? Tailoring your content to their preferences increases the likelihood of engagement.

Identifying Audience Pain Points, Interests, and Content Preferences

Understanding your audience's pain points, interests, and content preferences is crucial for creating content that resonates with them. This involves:

- Monitoring Conversations: Keep an eye on the conversations happening within your industry and among your followers. Use social listening tools like Hootsuite or

Brandwatch to track mentions, hashtags, and keywords related to your brand and industry.

- Engaging with Your Audience: Regularly interact with your audience through comments, direct messages, and polls. These interactions provide valuable feedback and insights into their preferences and needs.

- Analyzing Competitor Content: Study the content that your competitors are creating and see how their audience is responding. Identify the types of content that perform well and consider how you can adapt similar strategies to fit your brand.

By thoroughly understanding your audience, you can create content that speaks directly to their needs and interests, fostering deeper engagement and loyalty.

Types of Engaging Content

Different types of content can captivate your audience in various ways. Diversifying your content types keeps your audience interested and engaged.

The Power of Visual Content

Visual content is highly effective in capturing attention and driving engagement on social media. Humans process visual information faster than text, making visually appealing content more likely to stand out in crowded feeds.

- High-Quality Photos: Share high-quality photos that reflect your brand's aesthetic and values. Whether it's product photos, lifestyle shots, or behind-the-scenes glimpses, visually appealing images can enhance your brand's appeal.

- Videos: Videos are one of the most engaging types of content on social media. They can be used to tell stories, demonstrate products, or share valuable information. Short-form videos on platforms like TikTok and Instagram Reels can drive quick engagement, while longer videos on YouTube or IGTV can provide more in-depth content.

- Infographics: Infographics are an excellent way to present complex information in an easily digestible format. Use them to share statistics, tips, or process flows. Well-designed infographics can be highly shareable and help establish your brand as an authority in your industry.

Crafting Compelling Written Content

While visual content is powerful, well-crafted written content also plays a crucial role in engaging your audience. Engaging captions, storytelling posts, and informative blog articles can drive interaction and build a deeper connection with your followers.

- Engaging Captions: Pair your visual content with engaging captions that draw readers in and encourage interaction. Use captions to provide context, ask questions, or share anecdotes. A well-written caption can make your post more relatable and engaging.

- Storytelling Posts: Use storytelling to create emotional connections with your audience. Share personal stories, customer testimonials, or brand narratives that resonate with your followers. Storytelling helps humanize your brand and build trust with your audience.

- Informative Blog Articles: Create blog articles that provide valuable information to your audience. Whether it's how-to guides, industry insights, or thought leadership pieces, informative content can position your brand as an expert in your field. Blog articles also provide content that can be repurposed and shared across your social media platforms. We will discuss the importance of blogging in Chapter 8.

Utilizing Interactive Content to Boost Engagement

Interactive content encourages active participation from your audience, making them more likely to engage and share your posts.

- Polls and Quizzes: Use polls and quizzes to engage your audience and gather feedback. These formats are fun and easy for users to participate in, making them effective for driving engagement.

- Live Videos: Host live videos to interact with your audience in real-time. Live videos can be used for Q&A sessions, product demonstrations, or behind-the-scenes tours. They provide an opportunity for immediate interaction and create a sense of urgency and excitement.

- Stories and Highlights: Use Stories on platforms like Instagram and Facebook to share ephemeral content that disappears after 24 hours. Stories are great for sharing quick updates, behind-the-scenes content, and interactive features like polls and questions. Highlight important Stories on your profile to keep them accessible to your audience.

By diversifying your content types and tailoring them to your audience's preferences, you can create a more engaging and dynamic social media presence. The next chapter will delve into the art of storytelling and how to craft a compelling narrative that resonates with your audience.

Chapter 5: Leveraging Psychological Principles

Understanding and leveraging psychological principles can significantly enhance your social media strategy. By tapping into the ways people think and behave, you can create content that not only attracts attention but also drives engagement and action. In this chapter, we will explore key psychological principles and how to apply them to your social media efforts.

Reciprocity and Social Proof

Reciprocity and social proof are two powerful psychological principles that can drive social media engagement and build trust with your audience.

The Principle of Reciprocity: How Giving Value Encourages Followers to Engage and Reciprocate

The principle of reciprocity suggests that people feel obliged to return a favor when someone does something for them. On social media, this means that when you provide valuable content, your audience is more likely to reciprocate by engaging with your posts, sharing your content, or even making a purchase. Offering value can take many forms, such as educational posts, helpful tips, free resources, or entertaining content. When your audience perceives that they are gaining something of value, they are more likely to respond positively.

Building relationships is another crucial aspect of reciprocity. Engaging with your audience by responding to comments, answering questions, and showing appreciation for their support creates a sense of mutual respect. This encourages your followers to continue engaging with your content. Additionally, providing exclusive offers or content to your followers can enhance the feeling of reciprocity. This could include special discounts, early access to new products, or exclusive behind-the-scenes content.

Leveraging Social Proof: Using Testimonials, Reviews, and User-Generated Content to Build Credibility

Social proof is the idea that people look to the actions and opinions of others to determine what is correct or desirable. On social media, this can take the form of likes, shares, comments, testimonials, reviews, and user-generated content. Sharing positive testimonials and reviews from satisfied customers not only builds credibility but also reassures potential customers that others have had a positive experience with your brand.

Encouraging your followers to create and share content related to your brand can also act as social proof. User-generated content shows that real people use and enjoy your products or services, adding authenticity to your narrative. Reposting user-generated content helps build a sense of community and engagement. Highlighting high engagement metrics on your posts, such as the number of likes, comments, and shares, signals to new viewers that your content is valuable and popular, encouraging them to engage as well.

Incorporating Interactive Content to Boost Engagement

Interactive content, such as polls, questions, and quizzes, can significantly boost engagement on your profile. These tools invite your audience to participate actively, making them feel more involved and connected to your brand. For example, conducting polls to gather opinions on new products, content ideas, or industry topics provides valuable insights into your audience's preferences. Polls are quick and easy for followers to participate in, encouraging interaction.

Using question stickers or posts to invite your audience to ask you anything or share their thoughts on a specific topic drives engagement and gives you a chance to address their queries and build a stronger relationship. Quizzes are another form of interactive content that can be both fun and informative. They can educate your audience while engaging them in an interactive experience. By incorporating these interactive elements into your social media strategy, you can create a more dynamic and engaging profile that encourages ongoing interaction and builds stronger connections with your audience.

Case Studies and Examples

Consider how companies like Glossier and Starbucks effectively use interactive content. Glossier frequently uses Instagram polls and questions to gather feedback on new product ideas and engage with their audience. This makes followers feel like they are a part of the brand's decision-making process. Starbucks, on the other hand, uses seasonal quizzes and polls to engage their audience, especially around holiday promotions, driving both engagement and sales.

Advanced Strategies for Leveraging Reciprocity and Social Proof

Building a Referral Program

Creating a referral program that rewards your followers for bringing in new customers is an excellent way to leverage the principle of reciprocity. When followers refer friends and family to your brand, they feel they are doing a favor for both parties. Rewards can range from discounts to exclusive content or early access to new products.

Influencer Partnerships

Partnering with influencers who can provide authentic testimonials and reviews about your brand can amplify social proof. Influencers often have dedicated followers who trust their opinions, making their endorsements powerful. Ensure that these partnerships are genuine and that the influencers align with your brand values for the best results.

Customer Stories

Share detailed customer stories that highlight their journey and how your product or service made a difference in their lives. These stories should be relatable and showcase real people to maximize their impact. This not only builds social proof but also connects emotionally with your audience.

Scarcity and Urgency

Scarcity and urgency are powerful motivators that can drive immediate action from your audience. By creating a sense of limited availability or time-sensitive offers, you can encourage your followers to engage quickly.

Creating a Sense of Urgency: Limited-Time Offers, Flash Sales, and Exclusive Content

The principle of urgency suggests that people are more likely to take action when they feel they might miss out on an opportunity. Promoting limited-time discounts or promotions creates a sense of urgency and encourages quick action. Clearly communicating the deadline emphasizes the time-sensitive nature of the offer.

Flash sales, which last for a short period, such as 24 hours or even just a few hours, create a sense of urgency and encourage immediate purchases. The short duration makes the offer more appealing and prompts quick decisions. Offering exclusive content that is only available for a limited time, such as special reports, webinars, or behind-the-scenes videos, can also drive higher engagement. Highlighting the exclusivity and time-sensitive nature of the content can make it more desirable.

The Psychology of Scarcity: Why Limited Availability Increases Perceived Value

The principle of scarcity suggests that people place a higher value on items that are perceived to be scarce or in limited supply. Promoting products as being available in limited quantities can encourage customers to purchase before the item sells out. Highlighting that stock is running low can create a sense of urgency and drive immediate action.

Offering exclusive memberships or access to VIP groups that are limited in number can make these memberships more desirable. The exclusivity and limited availability increase the perceived value. Creating limited-edition products that are only available for a short time or in limited quantities also drives higher demand and engagement. The uniqueness and scarcity of these products make them more appealing to customers.

Practical Tips for Incorporating Scarcity and Urgency into Your Social Media Strategy

Using countdown timers in your posts or stories can visually emphasize the limited time available for an offer. This creates a sense of urgency and encourages immediate action. Clearly communicating what action you want your audience to take and why they need to act now is crucial. Using phrases like "limited time only," "while supplies last," or "don't miss out" creates urgency.

Making it clear when products are available in limited quantities, using phrases like "only a few left" or "selling fast," creates a sense of scarcity. Offering exclusive access to sales, content, or events for your followers can make them feel special and encourage them to take advantage of the opportunity. Promoting this exclusivity can drive higher engagement and build a stronger connection with your audience.

Leveraging Advanced Techniques for Scarcity and Urgency

Flash Sales with Tiered Discounts

Implement flash sales with tiered discounts that increase as the sale progresses. For example, offer a 10% discount for the first hour, 5% for the next two hours, and 2% for the remaining time. This encourages early action and maximizes engagement throughout the sale period.

Exclusive Content Drops

Tease exclusive content drops that are only available for a short period. This could include limited-edition products, exclusive webinars, or special reports. Announce these drops with a sense of excitement and urgency to drive immediate engagement.

Time-Limited Challenges

Create time-limited challenges or contests that encourage your audience to participate within a set timeframe. For example, challenge your followers to share their own content using your product with a specific hashtag within 48 hours for a chance to win a prize. This not only drives urgency but also generates user-generated content.

Building Community and Fostering Engagement

Creating a sense of community and fostering engagement are essential for building a loyal and active social media following. By focusing on these aspects, you can strengthen your relationship with your audience and encourage ongoing interaction.

Creating a Sense of Belonging

The need to belong is a fundamental human motivation. By creating a sense of community and belonging among your audience, you can build a loyal and engaged follower base. Using interactive content, such as polls, questions, and interactive posts, engages your audience and makes them feel involved. Encouraging them to share their opinions and experiences fosters a sense of community.

Creating spaces for your audience to connect with each other, such as Facebook Groups or forums, can foster deeper connections and a sense of belonging. These communities provide a platform for your audience to interact, share experiences, and support each other. Regular engagement with your audience by responding to comments, messages, and mentions shows appreciation for their support and creates a positive, welcoming environment.

Engaging with Your Audience

Engagement is a two-way street. By actively engaging with your audience, you can build stronger relationships and encourage more interaction. Taking the time to respond to comments and messages from your followers shows that you value their input and are willing to engage in conversation. This personal touch can make your audience feel valued and appreciated.

Hosting Q&A sessions, live videos, and AMAs (Ask Me Anything) allows you to interact with your audience in real-time. These sessions provide an opportunity for direct engagement and can build a sense of community. Personalized interactions, such as addressing your followers by

name and acknowledging their specific contributions or questions, can make your audience feel special and appreciated.

Collaborations with Other Profiles in Your Area

Collaborating with other profiles in your niche can expand your reach and introduce your brand to new audiences. Identifying potential collaborators who share a similar audience or have complementary expertise can be a strategic move. Reaching out to them with a clear proposal for collaboration can open up opportunities for joint ventures.

Collaborations can take many forms, including joint live sessions, co-created content, shoutouts, or giveaways. Choosing a format that aligns with your goals and resonates with your audience can maximize the impact of the collaboration. Looking at successful collaborations in your niche for inspiration can provide valuable insights. Analyzing what worked well and how you can adapt similar strategies for your brand can help you execute effective collaborations.

Building Long-Term Community Engagement

Creating Loyalty Programs

Develop loyalty programs that reward your most engaged followers. This could include exclusive access to new products, special discounts, or recognition on your social media profiles. Loyalty programs incentivize ongoing engagement and foster a sense of belonging.

Highlighting Community Members

Regularly highlight and celebrate your community members. Share user-generated content, feature follower stories, or create posts that recognize your most active followers. This not only shows appreciation but also encourages others to engage more.

Hosting Virtual Events

Organize virtual events such as webinars, workshops, or meet-and-greets. These events provide an opportunity for deeper engagement and allow your followers to connect with you and each other in a more meaningful way. Virtual events can strengthen community bonds and increase loyalty.

By understanding and leveraging psychological principles such as reciprocity, social proof, scarcity, and urgency, you can enhance your social media strategy and drive greater engagement. Building a sense of community and fostering ongoing interaction will further strengthen your relationship with your audience, creating a loyal and active follower base. The next chapter will delve into maximizing your reach on social media, including platform-specific strategies and understanding social media algorithms.

Chapter 6: Maximizing Your Reach

To maximize your reach on social media, it's essential to understand how social media algorithms work, the importance of early interaction, and platform-specific strategies. This chapter will delve into these aspects, providing you with actionable insights to enhance your social media presence and engagement.

Understanding Social Media Algorithms

Social media algorithms determine the visibility of your content in users' feeds. These algorithms prioritize content based on various factors, including engagement, relevance, and user behavior. Understanding how these algorithms work can help you optimize your content for maximum reach.

Social media platforms like Instagram, Facebook, Twitter, TikTok, and LinkedIn use complex algorithms to curate the content users see in their feeds. These algorithms are designed to enhance user experience by showing the most relevant and engaging content. For instance, Instagram's algorithm prioritizes posts that receive high engagement, assuming that if many people like, comment, and share a post, it must be valuable. Similarly, Facebook's algorithm considers factors such as user interactions, the type of content, and the recency of posts to determine what appears in the feed. Twitter, known for its real-time updates, prioritizes tweets based on relevance and engagement, while TikTok's algorithm focuses on user interactions and trending content to populate the For You page.

To create algorithm-friendly content, you need to focus on encouraging engagement. High engagement signals to the algorithm that your content is interesting and worth promoting. One effective strategy is to ask questions in your posts to prompt comments. For example, you could ask your followers for their opinions on a topic related to your industry or request feedback on a new product idea. You can also encourage shares by creating content that resonates emotionally or offers practical value, such as inspirational quotes, customer testimonials, or how-to guides.

Another tactic is to use visually appealing images and videos that attract likes and shares. High-quality visuals are more likely to catch users' attention as they scroll through their feeds. Consistency is also key; regularly posting high-quality content keeps your audience engaged and signals to the algorithm that you are an active user. Additionally, use relevant hashtags to increase the discoverability of your posts and reach a broader audience. For instance, if you're posting about a new tech gadget, using hashtags like #TechNews, #GadgetLover, and #Innovations can help attract users interested in technology.

Importance of Early Interaction

Early interaction is crucial for boosting the visibility of your posts. Social media algorithms often prioritize content that receives immediate engagement, as it signals to the platform that the content is relevant and interesting.

The first few hours after posting are critical for engagement. During this period, social media algorithms closely monitor how your post performs. High engagement shortly after posting can significantly increase your content's reach, as the algorithm will be more likely to show it to a broader audience. To maximize early engagement, it's essential to post when your audience is most active. Analyze your insights to determine the optimal times for posting, ensuring that your content reaches the maximum number of viewers. For example, if you notice that your audience is most active in the evenings, schedule your posts accordingly to maximize engagement.

Creating compelling headlines and thumbnails can also attract immediate attention and encourage users to engage with your content. An eye-catching thumbnail or an intriguing headline can make users stop scrolling and click on your post. Additionally, adding a compelling first comment to your post can set the tone for engagement and encourage others to comment. This technique is particularly effective on platforms like Instagram and Facebook, where the first comment often sets the context for the discussion.

Promoting your post across different platforms can also drive traffic and engagement. For example, you can share your Instagram post on your Facebook page, tweet about your new blog post, or link to your TikTok video on Instagram Stories. Cross-platform promotion helps you reach a wider audience and increases the chances of immediate interaction. However, it's important to customize your content for each platform rather than simply reposting the same content. Posting identical content across platforms can reduce your audience's incentive to follow you on multiple channels, as they will see the same thing everywhere. Tailoring your content to fit the unique strengths and user preferences of each platform can help maintain interest and engagement across all your social media accounts.

Examining successful examples can provide insights and inspiration for your strategy. National Geographic, for instance, often posts stunning images with engaging captions that ask questions or share intriguing facts. This approach encourages immediate likes and comments, boosting the post's visibility. Starbucks frequently uses Instagram Stories and polls to engage their audience quickly. By asking questions about favorite drinks or new product ideas, they generate immediate responses and interactions. BuzzFeed effectively uses Twitter to drive early engagement. By posting catchy headlines and using trending hashtags, they attract immediate attention and retweets. These examples demonstrate how early interaction can significantly enhance your content's reach and engagement.

Common Strategies for All Platforms

While each social media platform has its unique characteristics and user behaviors, there are common strategies that can enhance your reach and engagement across all platforms. Implementing these strategies ensures a consistent and effective social media presence.

Internal Linking

Internal linking refers to the practice of linking your content across different posts and pages within the same platform or across your different social media accounts. This strategy helps keep your audience engaged by directing them to related content. For example, on Instagram, you can use Stories to link to your latest post or use the "Swipe Up" feature (for accounts with over 10,000 followers) to link to external content like blog posts or products. On YouTube, you can use end screens and cards to promote other videos on your channel, increasing watch time and engagement.

Engagement

Engagement is a critical factor that social media algorithms consider when determining the visibility of your content.

Engaging with your audience by responding to comments, liking user-generated content, and participating in discussions can significantly boost your visibility. Encouraging your followers to interact with your content through likes, shares, comments, and saves signals to the algorithm that your content is valuable and relevant.

Consistency

Consistency in posting helps maintain your audience's interest and signals to social media algorithms that you are an active user. Developing a content calendar can help you plan and schedule your posts in advance, ensuring that you post regularly without overwhelming your audience. Consistent branding, including visual elements like colors and logos, and a consistent tone of voice, also reinforces your brand identity and makes your content more recognizable.

Quality Content

Quality content is essential for keeping your audience engaged and attracting new followers. High-quality images, well-produced videos, and well-written posts capture attention and encourage interaction. Investing in good equipment, using professional editing software, and taking the time to create thoughtful, valuable content can set you apart from the competition.

Calls to Action (CTAs)

Incorporating clear and compelling calls to action in your posts can drive engagement and conversions. Whether you want your audience to like, comment, share, visit your website, or make a purchase, a well-crafted CTA can guide them towards the desired action. Use action-oriented language and create a sense of urgency to encourage immediate response.

Platform-Specific Insights

Each social media platform has unique characteristics and user behaviors. Understanding these nuances can help you tailor your content and maximize your reach on each platform.

Instagram is a visual platform that prioritizes high-quality images and videos. It favors engagement through likes, comments, and shares, but also values saves and story interactions. To maximize reach on Instagram, use a mix of content types, including posts, Stories, Reels, and IGTV. Each format has its own engagement benefits and can help you reach different segments of your audience. For example, Stories offer a way to share more casual, ephemeral content, while Reels can help you reach a wider audience with short, engaging videos. Leveraging Instagram Stories with interactive elements like polls, questions, and quizzes can also boost engagement. Using relevant and trending hashtags increases discoverability, helping your content reach users who are interested in those topics.

Additionally, Instagram's algorithm favors posts that receive a high level of engagement shortly after being posted. To leverage this, consider posting during peak times when your audience is most active. Engaging with your audience through comments and direct messages can also signal to the algorithm that your content is engaging and relevant. Consistency in posting and maintaining a cohesive aesthetic can further enhance your brand's presence on the platform.

TikTok is known for its short, engaging videos that often feature trending sounds and challenges. The platform favors creativity and trends, making it ideal for viral content. To succeed on TikTok, create short, creative videos that capture attention quickly. Incorporating popular sounds and participating in trending challenges can boost your video's chances of being featured on the For You page. TikTok's algorithm considers hashtag trends when recommending videos to users, so using relevant hashtags is essential. Additionally, tailoring your content to appeal to a younger audience, which dominates TikTok, can increase engagement and reach.

One of TikTok's strengths is its ability to make content go viral quickly. To capitalize on this, keep your videos concise and engaging from the very first second. Use eye-catching visuals and engaging storytelling techniques to hold viewers' attention. Collaborating with popular TikTok influencers or participating in trending challenges can also increase your visibility. Regularly updating your content and experimenting with different formats can help you stay relevant on the platform.

Facebook is a versatile platform suitable for a wide range of content types, including text updates, photos, videos, and links. It values engagement through likes, comments, and shares, and also prioritizes content from close connections and groups. To maximize reach on Facebook, share a variety of content types and use Facebook Live for real-time engagement. Creating and participating in Facebook Groups can help build a sense of community and drive higher engagement. Encouraging interactions by asking questions, creating polls, and sharing content that prompts discussion can also boost your content's visibility. Understanding your audience's preferences through Facebook Insights allows you to tailor your content strategy effectively.

Facebook's algorithm prioritizes content that encourages meaningful interactions between users. To leverage this, focus on creating content that sparks conversations and prompts users to share their thoughts. Hosting live sessions can also drive real-time engagement and create a sense of immediacy. Additionally, using Facebook's advertising tools can help you reach a broader audience and target specific demographics. Regularly analyzing your performance metrics can help you refine your strategy and improve your content's effectiveness.

Twitter/X is characterized by its fast-paced, real-time nature. It's ideal for sharing short updates, news, and engaging in conversations. The platform's user base is varied, with a strong presence of professionals, influencers, and news organizations. To maximize reach on Twitter, share concise updates, news, and engage in conversations. Using Twitter threads to tell longer stories and provide more in-depth content can also be effective. Participating in trending topics and using relevant hashtags can increase your content's discoverability and reach a broader audience. Engaging with your followers by responding to comments and joining discussions can build a stronger connection with your audience.

Twitter's algorithm favors tweets that receive high engagement quickly. To leverage this, post during peak times when your followers are most active. Use engaging visuals, such as images and videos, to make your tweets stand out. Participating in trending conversations and using popular hashtags can increase your visibility. Engaging with influencers and thought leaders in your industry can also amplify your reach and enhance your credibility on the platform.

LinkedIn is focused on professional networking and is best for sharing industry insights, professional achievements, and thought leadership content. Its user base consists mainly of professionals and businesses, making it an ideal platform for B2B marketing and professional branding. To maximize reach on LinkedIn, share professional insights and industry-related content. Using LinkedIn Articles and posts to provide in-depth information can position you as a thought leader in your industry. Engaging with your network through comments and messages can build professional relationships and increase your visibility. Understanding LinkedIn's user demographics and tailoring your content to appeal to professionals can enhance your engagement and reach.

LinkedIn's algorithm prioritizes content that fosters professional conversations and connections. To leverage this, focus on sharing valuable insights and industry trends that encourage discussion. Engaging with your network by commenting on their posts and participating in relevant groups can increase your visibility. Using LinkedIn's publishing platform to share long-form content, such as articles and whitepapers, can further establish your expertise. Regularly updating your profile and showcasing your achievements can also enhance your professional presence on the platform.

YouTube is a video-centric platform that prioritizes high-quality, engaging videos. The algorithm considers factors such as watch time, engagement (likes, comments, shares), and video relevance to determine which videos to recommend. To maximize reach on YouTube, create compelling video content that captures viewers' attention within the first few seconds. Use eye-catching thumbnails and intriguing titles to attract clicks. Encourage viewers to like, comment, and subscribe to your channel, as these interactions signal to the algorithm that your content is engaging.

Consistency in posting is crucial on YouTube. Develop a regular posting schedule to keep your audience engaged and encourage them to return for new content. Utilize YouTube's features, such as end screens and cards, to promote other videos on your channel and increase watch time. Engaging with your viewers through comments and community posts can also build a loyal audience and enhance your channel's visibility.

Threads is a newer platform from Instagram, designed for more intimate sharing among close friends. The content shared on Threads is highly personalized and often less polished than on main social media feeds. To maximize reach on Threads, focus on creating authentic, behind-the-scenes content that gives your audience a closer look at your daily life or business operations. Engage with your audience through direct messages and personalized interactions to build a strong sense of community.

Since Threads is closely linked to Instagram, promoting your Threads content on Instagram can help drive traffic between the two platforms. Encourage your followers to join you on Threads for exclusive updates and content that they won't see on your main Instagram feed.

Snapchat is known for its ephemeral content and youthful user base. The platform favors short, engaging snaps and stories that capture attention quickly. To maximize reach on Snapchat, create visually appealing and concise content that resonates with a younger audience. Utilize features like lenses, filters, and geotags to make your snaps more engaging and interactive.

Building a consistent presence on Snapchat can help you stay top of mind with your audience. Engage with your followers by responding to their snaps and messages, and encourage them to interact with your content. Promoting your Snapchat account on other social media platforms can also help drive traffic and increase your reach.

Tailoring Content for Each Platform

While it might seem convenient to post the same content across all platforms, this approach can actually hurt your social media strategy. Different platforms have unique audiences, content preferences, and engagement patterns. Therefore, it's crucial to tailor your content for each platform to maximize engagement and reach.

Why Reposting the Same Content Can Hurt Your Strategy

When you repost the same content across all platforms, you risk making your audience feel like they're seeing the same thing everywhere. This reduces their incentive to follow you on multiple channels, as there is no added value in doing so. Each platform has its own culture and expectations, and what works on one platform might not resonate on another. For example, a highly polished promotional video might perform well on YouTube but could feel out of place on a more casual and spontaneous platform like Snapchat.

Tailoring Your Content to Fit Each Platform

To effectively engage your audience across different platforms, customize your content to align with the unique characteristics and user behaviors of each platform. Here are some tips:

- Instagram: Focus on high-quality visuals, engaging captions, and interactive elements like polls and questions. Use Stories and Reels for behind-the-scenes content and short, engaging videos.

- TikTok: Create short, creative videos that incorporate trending sounds and challenges. Keep your content fun, spontaneous, and visually appealing to capture the attention of TikTok's younger audience.

- Facebook: Share a mix of content types, including text updates, photos, videos, and links. Use Facebook Live for real-time engagement and create and participate in Facebook Groups to build a sense of community.

- Twitter/X: Share concise updates, news, and engage in conversations. Use Twitter threads to tell longer stories and provide more in-depth content. Participate in trending topics and use relevant hashtags to increase visibility.

- LinkedIn: Share professional insights, industry-related content, and thought leadership articles. Engage with your network through comments and messages and participate in relevant groups to increase visibility.

- YouTube: Create high-quality, engaging videos with compelling thumbnails and titles. Develop a regular posting schedule and use features like end screens and cards to promote other videos on your channel.

- Threads: Share authentic, behind-the-scenes content that gives your audience a closer look at your daily life or business operations. Engage with your audience through direct messages and personalized interactions.

- Snapchat: Create short, visually appealing snaps and stories that resonate with a younger audience. Utilize features like lenses, filters, and geotags to make your content more engaging and interactive.

By tailoring your content to fit the unique strengths and user preferences of each platform, you can maintain interest and engagement across all your social media accounts. The next chapter will explore the power of blogging for social media and SEO, and how integrating blogs with your social media strategy can enhance your overall online presence.

Chapter 7: The Power of Blogging for Social Media

Blogging is a powerful tool that can significantly enhance your social media strategy. This chapter explores how integrating blogs with your social media presence can drive engagement, increase visibility, and help establish your online identity.

Boosting Your Social Media Presence with Blogs

Blogging can serve as the backbone of your social media content, providing a steady stream of valuable information that you can share across your platforms. High-quality blog content not only engages your audience but also positions you as a knowledgeable and credible source in your field.

Creating Shareable Content

One of the primary benefits of blogging is the ability to create shareable content that drives engagement on social media. Shareable content is informative, entertaining, or inspiring and encourages your audience to share it with their networks. To create shareable blog content, focus on addressing common questions and pain points within your industry. For instance, if you run a fitness blog, you could write posts on topics like "10 Quick Workouts for Busy Professionals" or "How to Maintain a Healthy Diet on a Budget."

In addition to valuable information, make your blog posts visually appealing by including high-quality images, infographics, and videos. Visual elements not only enhance the reader's experience but also make the content more shareable. Use compelling headlines and introductions to grab the reader's attention and keep them engaged throughout the post. Engaging introductions set the tone for the rest of the post and entice readers to continue reading.

Driving Traffic from Social Media to Your Blog

Sharing your blog posts on social media is an effective way to drive traffic to your website. Each blog post provides an opportunity to promote your content across various platforms, increasing its reach and engagement. When sharing your blog posts, tailor the message to fit each platform's unique characteristics. For example, create a visually appealing graphic with a quote or key takeaway for Instagram, a concise and engaging summary for Twitter, and a more detailed introduction for Facebook.

Encourage your followers to visit your blog by including clear calls to action (CTAs) in your social media posts. Phrases like "Read more on our blog" or "Check out the full article here" can prompt your audience to click through to your website. Additionally, using relevant hashtags can increase the discoverability of your posts and attract users who are interested in your content.

Establishing Your Online Identity

Regularly publishing high-quality blog content can help establish your online identity. Sharing insights, expertise, and innovative ideas through your blog shows your audience that you are knowledgeable and trustworthy. By consistently delivering valuable content, you can build trust and credibility with your followers.

To build your online identity, focus on writing in-depth, well-researched blog posts that address complex topics within your industry. Share your unique perspectives and experiences, and provide actionable advice that your audience can apply. Engage with your readers by responding to comments and encouraging discussions on your blog and social media platforms. This interaction not only builds community but also shows your audience that you are approachable and willing to share your expertise.

Combining Blogs with Social Media for Maximum Impact

Integrating your blog content with your social media strategy can amplify your reach and engagement, driving more traffic to your website and increasing your online visibility.

Best Practices for Promoting Blog Content on Social Media

To effectively promote your blog content on social media, use eye-catching visuals, compelling headlines, and clear CTAs. Create custom graphics or videos for each platform to make your posts stand out in users' feeds. Tailor your messaging to fit the tone and style of each platform, ensuring that it resonates with your audience.

For example, on Instagram, you can create a carousel post with highlights from your blog post, while on LinkedIn, you can share a more detailed summary with key takeaways. Encourage your followers to share your blog posts by making it easy for them to do so. Include social sharing buttons on your blog and use hashtags to increase the discoverability of your social media posts.

Cross-Platform Strategies to Increase Visibility and Drive Traffic

Cross-platform promotion involves sharing your blog content across multiple social media channels to maximize its reach. When promoting your blog posts, consider the unique strengths of each platform and tailor your approach accordingly. For instance, use Instagram Stories to share behind-the-scenes content related to your blog post, create a Twitter thread to break down the main points, and host a Facebook Live session to discuss the topic in more detail.

Additionally, consider collaborating with influencers or industry experts to amplify your reach. Guest blogging and co-hosting webinars or live sessions can introduce your content to new audiences and drive more traffic to your website.

Case Studies of Businesses Successfully Using Blogs and Social Media Together

Examining successful case studies can provide valuable insights and inspiration for your own strategy. For example, Buffer, a social media management tool, effectively uses its blog to drive traffic and generate leads. By consistently publishing high-quality, engaging content and promoting it across social media, Buffer has established itself as a trusted resource in the social media marketing industry.

Buffer's blog covers a wide range of topics related to social media marketing, content creation, and productivity. The company uses a mix of how-to guides, case studies, and research-backed articles to provide value to its readers. Buffer also promotes its blog posts on social media platforms like Twitter, Facebook, and LinkedIn, tailoring the content to fit each platform's unique audience. By integrating its blog content with its social media strategy, Buffer has built a loyal community of followers and increased brand visibility.

Additional Strategies for Maximizing Blog and Social Media Integration

Email Marketing

In addition to social media, email marketing can be a powerful tool to drive traffic to your blog. Building an email list allows you to directly reach your audience with new blog posts, updates, and exclusive content. Encourage your social media followers to subscribe to your email list by offering incentives such as free resources, discounts, or exclusive content.

Once you have an email list, regularly send out newsletters that highlight your latest blog posts and encourage subscribers to visit your website. Personalize your emails to make them more engaging and relevant to your audience. Use compelling subject lines and preview text to entice recipients to open your emails and click through to your blog.

SEO and Analytics Tools

Utilizing SEO and analytics tools can help you optimize your blog content and measure its performance. Tools like Google Analytics, SEMrush, and Ahrefs provide insights into your website's traffic, user behavior, and keyword rankings. Use these tools to identify which blog posts are performing well and which areas need improvement.

Regularly monitor your blog's performance and adjust your content strategy based on the data. Identify high-performing keywords and create more content around those topics. Analyze your traffic sources to see which social media platforms are driving the most traffic to your blog and focus your efforts on those channels.

Engaging with Your Audience

Engagement is key to building a loyal audience and driving traffic to your blog. Respond to comments on your blog posts and social media platforms to show your audience that you value their input. Encourage discussions and ask for feedback to create a sense of community.

Hosting live Q&A sessions, webinars, or interactive social media posts can also drive engagement and promote your blog content. Use these opportunities to address common questions and provide additional value to your audience. Engaging with your audience helps build trust and loyalty, making them more likely to share your content and return to your blog.

By combining the power of blogging with a robust social media strategy, you can enhance your online presence, drive engagement, and establish your online identity. The next chapter will explore the value of sharing knowledge to build trust and how creating educational content can drive engagement and establish your brand as a trusted source.

Chapter 8: Sharing Knowledge to Build Trust

Sharing knowledge is one of the most effective ways to build trust and credibility with your audience. When you provide valuable information and insights, you demonstrate your expertise and create a sense of reliability. This chapter will explore how sharing knowledge can drive engagement and help establish your online identity.

The Value of Sharing Information

Sharing valuable information can significantly boost your credibility and establish you as an authority in your field.

Many professionals hesitate to share their expertise for fear of giving away too much, but in reality, sharing knowledge builds trust and attracts a loyal audience. This section will delve into why sharing information is essential for building trust and how it can enhance your online presence.

Building trust through knowledge sharing is a cornerstone of establishing a robust online presence. When you openly share your knowledge, your audience begins to see you as a reliable source of information. This trust encourages them to return to your content repeatedly and recommend it to others. For example, an attorney might write blog posts about the basics of the music industry, explaining common legal issues artists face and how to navigate them. This not only helps the audience but also positions the attorney as an expert in the field. Similarly, a mechanic might create videos detailing the causes of common car noises and how to diagnose them. While some might worry that this would lead potential customers to fix their own cars, it often has the opposite effect. People appreciate the mechanic's expertise and transparency, leading them to trust the mechanic with more complex repairs.

The idea of sharing valuable information and knowledge is not new, but its significance has grown in the digital age. Transparency and accessibility to information are now key factors that can distinguish you from your competitors. When you share your expertise, you provide immediate value to your audience, which fosters a deeper connection and builds loyalty over time. The internet is filled with information, but much of it is generic or shallow. By offering detailed, high-quality content, you not only meet the immediate needs of your audience but also demonstrate your commitment to their growth and success.

Moreover, sharing information can lead to increased engagement on your social media platforms. When your audience finds value in your content, they are more likely to interact with it by liking, commenting, and sharing. This engagement can significantly boost your visibility and reach on social media, as algorithms favor content that generates high levels of interaction.

Additionally, engaged followers are more likely to become loyal customers who trust your brand and are willing to invest in your products or services.

Sharing knowledge also positions you as a thought leader in your industry. By consistently providing valuable insights and staying ahead of industry trends, you establish yourself as a go-to resource for information. This not only attracts a dedicated audience but also opens up opportunities for collaborations, speaking engagements, and other professional advancements. Thought leadership can elevate your brand and create a lasting impact on your audience, ensuring long-term success and growth.

Overcoming the Fear of Sharing Too Much

Many professionals fear that sharing their knowledge will lead to a loss of business, as people might choose to do things themselves rather than seek professional help. However, this fear is often unfounded. Sharing valuable information shows your expertise and builds trust, making people more likely to seek your services when they need professional help. This section will address the common concerns associated with sharing knowledge and explain why these fears are typically misplaced.

The concern that sharing knowledge will result in a loss of business is understandable but often misguided. When people come across content that is genuinely helpful and insightful, they tend to appreciate the source more. This appreciation can translate into increased loyalty and trust, which are critical for long-term business relationships. For instance, a digital marketing consultant who shares free, detailed tutorials on SEO techniques may initially fear that potential clients will use the information to handle their SEO themselves. However, these potential clients are more likely to realize the complexity and expertise required and thus prefer to hire the consultant for professional services. The key is to provide just enough information to help your audience while still highlighting the value of your professional services.

Sharing knowledge does not mean giving away all your secrets. Instead, it involves providing valuable insights and practical advice that can help your audience solve problems and achieve their goals. By doing so, you demonstrate your expertise and establish yourself as a trusted authority in your field. This trust can lead to increased business opportunities, as potential clients are more likely to seek your services when they need professional help. Moreover, sharing knowledge can help you build a loyal community of followers who appreciate your transparency and willingness to share valuable information.

One way to address the fear of sharing too much is to strike a balance between free content and premium services. You can offer valuable information for free while reserving more in-depth, personalized, or advanced insights for your paying clients. This approach allows you to demonstrate your expertise and build trust with your audience while still maintaining a revenue stream from your premium services. By providing a taste of your knowledge, you entice potential clients to seek your paid services for more comprehensive and personalized solutions.

Another strategy to overcome the fear of sharing too much is to focus on the benefits of building a loyal and engaged audience. When you share valuable information, you attract a dedicated following who trust and respect your expertise. This loyal audience is more likely to support your business by purchasing your products or services, recommending you to others, and engaging with your content. In the long run, the benefits of building a loyal and engaged audience far outweigh the potential risks of sharing knowledge.

In conclusion, sharing knowledge is a powerful way to build trust and establish your online identity. By addressing the fear of sharing too much and focusing on the long-term benefits, you can leverage your expertise to attract a loyal audience and grow your business. The next section will explore how to create educational content that engages your audience and establishes your authority.

Creating Educational Content

Educational content is a powerful way to engage your audience and establish your authority. By providing practical, useful information, you can help your audience solve problems and achieve their goals, which in turn builds loyalty and trust. This section will provide a detailed guide on creating educational content that resonates with your audience and positions you as an expert in your field.

To create effective educational content, start by identifying the key topics and areas of expertise that are most relevant to your audience. Think about the questions your audience frequently asks, the challenges they face, and the topics that generate the most interest. Conducting surveys, engaging in social media discussions, and analyzing comments and feedback can provide valuable insights into what your audience wants to learn. For instance, if you are a personal trainer, your audience might be interested in topics such as workout routines, nutrition advice, and injury prevention. By focusing on these areas, you can create content that addresses their needs and interests.

Understanding your audience's needs is crucial for creating content that resonates.

If you can anticipate their questions and concerns, you can craft content that directly addresses these points. This not only helps your audience but also positions you as a proactive and attentive professional. For example, if you notice that many of your followers on social media are asking about beginner workout routines, creating a series of blog posts or videos on this topic can be highly effective. Each piece of content can build on the last, creating a comprehensive guide that your audience will find invaluable.

Presenting information in an engaging and accessible manner is crucial for keeping your audience interested and ensuring they understand and retain the information. Use visuals such as images, infographics, and videos to make your content more engaging and easier to understand. Visual aids can help illustrate complex concepts and keep your audience's attention. Tell stories to make your content more relatable and memorable. Sharing real-life examples and case studies can help your audience see how the information applies to their own situations. Break down information into smaller, digestible sections with clear headings and subheadings. This makes it easier for your audience to follow and absorb the information. Include actionable tips that your audience can implement immediately. This helps them see the value of your content and encourages them to return for more.

The way you present your content can significantly impact its effectiveness. Visual content is particularly powerful because it can make complex information easier to understand and more engaging. For instance, if you are explaining a complicated financial concept, using an infographic to break down the information into visual segments can make it much more digestible. Similarly, video content can be very effective for demonstrating techniques or processes. A cooking blog, for example, might use step-by-step videos to show how to prepare a dish, making it easier for viewers to follow along and replicate the recipe.

Educational content can drive engagement by encouraging your audience to interact with your content and share it with others. Create interactive content such as quizzes, polls, and Q&A sessions to engage your audience and encourage participation. For example, you could create a quiz to help your audience determine their fitness level or a poll to gather feedback on what topics they want to learn about next. Host live sessions such as webinars, live streams, or Instagram Live events to provide real-time education and engage with your audience directly. Live sessions allow for immediate interaction and can create a sense of community. Share educational snippets and tips on your social media platforms to provide continuous value and keep your audience engaged. For example, you could post a daily fitness tip on Instagram or share a short how-to video on TikTok.

Interactive content is particularly effective because it transforms passive consumption into active participation. When your audience engages with a quiz, poll, or live session, they are not just receiving information—they are interacting with it and with you. This interaction can build a stronger connection and a more engaged community. For example, if you are a nutritionist, hosting a live Q&A session where followers can ask questions about healthy eating can provide immense value. It allows you to address specific concerns in real-time and shows that you are accessible and responsive.

The Principle of Reciprocity

The principle of reciprocity is a key psychological concept that explains why sharing knowledge builds trust. Reciprocity is the social norm of responding to a positive action with another positive action, rewarding kind actions. When you give something of value, such as useful information or helpful advice, people feel an inherent obligation to reciprocate. This can be in the form of loyalty, trust, or even business.

In the context of social media and content marketing, when you freely share your expertise, your audience feels grateful and more inclined to engage with your content, share it with others, and even seek out your services or products. This principle is deeply rooted in human psychology and is a powerful tool for building strong, trust-based relationships with your audience.

For instance, if you are a fitness trainer and you offer free workout tips and nutrition advice through your blog and social media channels, your audience will appreciate the value you provide. This appreciation can translate into increased engagement, as your followers are more likely to comment on your posts, share your content, and recommend you to others. Over time, this builds a sense of loyalty and trust, making them more likely to choose you as their fitness trainer when they need professional help.

The principle of reciprocity is not about giving away everything for free but rather about providing enough value to build trust and demonstrate your expertise. This builds a foundation for a strong relationship where your audience feels valued and understood, which in turn fosters loyalty and long-term engagement.

Reciprocity also encourages a cycle of positive interactions. When you give something valuable to your audience, they feel compelled to reciprocate in some way. This could be through social media engagement, word-of-mouth referrals, or even becoming paying customers. The more you give, the more you build a community that supports and promotes your brand. This cycle of giving and receiving creates a sustainable model for growth and success in the digital age.

Moreover, the principle of reciprocity can extend beyond your immediate audience. When your followers share your valuable content, they introduce new people to your brand, expanding your reach organically. This extended reach not only brings in potential new followers but also reinforces your authority and credibility in your field. The ripple effect of reciprocity can significantly enhance your brand's visibility and reputation over time.

Case Studies and Examples

Examining real-life examples can provide valuable insights into how sharing knowledge can build trust and drive engagement. For instance, Neil Patel, a renowned digital marketing expert, shares extensive knowledge through his blog, videos, and social media. By providing detailed guides, tips, and case studies, he has built a loyal following and established himself as a trusted authority in digital marketing. Patel's willingness to share his expertise and insights freely has not only built his brand but also attracted numerous clients who seek his professional services.

Neil Patel's journey in digital marketing started with a genuine desire to help businesses grow by understanding the intricacies of online marketing. He began by sharing detailed, actionable insights through his blog, focusing on topics such as SEO, content marketing, and social media strategies. His blog posts are often comprehensive guides that break down complex concepts into manageable steps, making it easier for readers to implement his advice. By consistently providing high-quality content, Neil has built a reputation for being a reliable source of information in the digital marketing industry.

In addition to his blog, Neil uses other mediums such as YouTube videos, podcasts, and social media posts to share his knowledge. His transparency and willingness to share valuable insights have earned him a large following across multiple platforms. This multi-channel approach not only broadens his reach but also reinforces his expertise. By giving away substantial value for free, Neil has demonstrated the principle of reciprocity. His audience feels a sense of gratitude and trust, which translates into loyalty and a preference for his services when they need professional digital marketing assistance. This strategy has allowed Neil to attract and retain clients who appreciate his depth of knowledge and are willing to invest in his expertise.

Another excellent example is Dr. Sandra Lee, also known as Dr. Pimple Popper. Dr. Lee gained widespread recognition by sharing educational and entertaining content about skincare and dermatology on social media and YouTube. Her transparency and willingness to share her expertise have built a large, loyal following. People appreciate her approachable manner and in-depth knowledge, which has led to a significant increase in her clinic's visibility and patient base.

Dr. Lee's approach to content creation involves a mix of educational posts, entertaining videos, and personal interactions. She often shares detailed explanations of various skin conditions, treatments, and preventive measures. Her videos, which show her performing procedures, are not only informative but also satisfy a certain curiosity that many viewers have. This unique blend of education and entertainment has made her content highly shareable and engaging.

Moreover, Dr. Lee frequently engages with her audience through Q&A sessions, live videos, and social media comments. This direct interaction helps her build a personal connection with her followers, making them feel valued and heard. By consistently providing valuable content and engaging with her audience, Dr. Lee has effectively utilized the principle of reciprocity. Her followers feel a sense of gratitude and trust, which has translated into increased business for her clinic. The success of Dr. Lee's online presence highlights the importance of combining valuable content with genuine engagement to build a loyal and trusting audience.

These examples highlight the importance of transparency and accessibility in building an online presence. By offering valuable insights and practical advice, you can demonstrate your expertise and build a loyal audience. Both Neil Patel and Dr. Sandra Lee have shown that sharing knowledge does not diminish their business but rather enhances it by establishing them as go-to sources in their respective fields.

Conclusion

Sharing knowledge is a powerful way to build trust and credibility with your audience. By providing valuable, educational content, you demonstrate your expertise and create a sense of reliability. This not only engages your audience but also helps establish your online identity as a trusted source of information. The next chapter will explore how to analyze and adapt your strategy based on feedback and performance metrics to ensure continuous improvement and success in your social media efforts.

By focusing on creating and sharing high-quality educational content, you can build a strong online presence and a loyal audience. Your willingness to share your expertise will set you apart as a trusted and valuable resource in your field. This approach not only enhances your credibility but also drives engagement and fosters a deeper connection with your audience.

Chapter 9: Analyzing and Adapting Your Strategy

In the rapidly changing landscape of social media, it is crucial to continuously analyze and adapt your strategy. This chapter will delve into the importance of monitoring your performance, using feedback to refine your approach, and remaining flexible to ensure ongoing success.

Monitoring Your Performance

To effectively manage your social media presence, you need to regularly monitor your performance. This involves tracking key metrics that provide insights into how your content is performing and how your audience is engaging with it. Monitoring your performance helps you understand what is working, what isn't, and where you can make improvements.

Start by identifying the key metrics that are most relevant to your goals. These metrics might include engagement rates, such as likes, comments, and shares, as well as reach and impressions, which indicate how many people are seeing your content. For instance, if your goal is to increase brand awareness, you might focus on reach and impressions. If your goal is to foster a community, engagement metrics will be more important.

Key Metrics Across Different Platforms

Understanding the key metrics across various social media platforms is crucial for effectively analyzing your performance and refining your strategy. Each platform has its unique set of metrics that you should be familiar with to gauge your success accurately. Here are the key terms and what they mean for the major social media platforms:

Facebook

1. Reach: The number of unique users who have seen your post. This metric helps you understand the breadth of your content's visibility.

2. Impressions: The total number of times your post has been displayed, regardless of clicks. This includes multiple views by the same users.

3. Engagement Rate: The percentage of people who engaged with your content (likes, comments, shares) out of those who saw it. A higher engagement rate indicates more effective content.

4. Clicks: The number of times users clicked on links in your post. This measures how compelling your call-to-action is.

5. Reactions: The range of emotions (like, love, haha, wow, sad, angry) users express about your post. Understanding reactions can provide insights into how your content resonates emotionally with your audience.

Instagram

1. Reach: The number of unique accounts that have seen your post. This metric indicates the potential audience size for your content.

2. Impressions: The total number of times your post has been seen, including multiple views by the same accounts.

3. Engagement Rate: The percentage of people who interacted with your post (likes, comments, saves) out of those who saw it. This is a critical metric for assessing the effectiveness of your content.

4. Saves: The number of times users saved your post to revisit later. This metric shows how valuable your content is to your audience.

5. Story Views: The number of views each segment of your Instagram Stories receives. High story views can indicate strong follower interest and engagement.

6. Shares: The number of times users share your post with others through direct messages or their own stories. Shares are crucial for organic growth and reaching new audiences.

Twitter/X

1. Impressions: The number of times your tweet has been seen. This includes views on the Twitter timeline and in search results.

2. Engagements: The total number of interactions (likes, retweets, replies, clicks) with your tweet. This metric shows how well your content is engaging your audience.

3. Engagement Rate: The percentage of engagements per impressions. A higher engagement rate suggests your content is highly relevant to your audience.

4. Retweets: The number of times your tweet has been shared by others. Retweets help increase your content's visibility and reach.

5. Mentions: The number of times other users have tagged your handle in their tweets. Mentions can indicate how often your brand is being discussed on the platform.

LinkedIn

1. Impressions: The number of times your post has been seen by users. This metric helps gauge the initial exposure of your content.

2. Clicks: The number of times users clicked on your content, company name, or logo. Clicks indicate interest in your content and brand.

3. Engagement Rate: The number of interactions (likes, comments, shares) divided by the number of impressions. A high engagement rate suggests that your content is resonating well with your audience.

4. Followers: The number of people following your company page. Growth in followers indicates increasing interest in your brand.

5. CTR (Click-Through Rate): The percentage of clicks out of the total impressions. A higher CTR means your content is compelling enough to drive action.

TikTok

1. Views: The number of times your video has been watched. This is a primary metric for gauging the popularity of your content.

2. Likes: The number of times users liked your video. Likes are a basic form of engagement and indicate approval of your content.

3. Shares: The number of times users shared your video with others. Shares are vital for increasing the reach of your content beyond your immediate followers.

4. Comments: The number of comments on your video. Comments can provide direct feedback and engagement from your audience.

5. Watch Time: The total amount of time viewers spent watching your video. High watch time suggests that your content is engaging and retaining viewers.

6. Engagement Rate: The sum of interactions (likes, comments, shares) divided by the number of views. A high engagement rate indicates that your content is resonating well with viewers.

The Importance of Key Metrics

Each of these metrics offers valuable insights into how your content is performing and how your audience is interacting with it. For example, on Instagram, shares are particularly important because they help amplify your content's reach organically. When users share your posts, they expose your content to their followers, which can significantly increase your visibility and attract new followers. Similarly, high engagement rates on any platform indicate that your content is relevant and interesting to your audience, which can help you tailor future content to better meet their preferences.

By understanding and tracking these key metrics, you can make informed decisions about your social media strategy, optimize your content for better performance, and ultimately achieve your goals more effectively.

Using Analytics Tools

Use social media analytics tools to gather data on these metrics. Most social media platforms, such as Facebook, Instagram, and Twitter, offer built-in analytics that provide a wealth of information about your performance. Tools like Google Analytics can also provide insights into how your social media efforts are driving traffic to your website. By regularly reviewing these analytics, you can gain a deeper understanding of your audience's behavior and preferences.

Third-Party Analytics Tools

While built-in analytics tools are beneficial, there are also several third-party applications available that offer more advanced analytics features. Platforms like

Sprout Social, Hootsuite, and Buffer provide comprehensive analytics that go beyond the basics provided by social media platforms. These tools can offer detailed reports on audience demographics, engagement trends, and content performance. However, it is essential to be cautious when using these third-party tools.

Many third-party applications estimate analytics data that isn't directly available from social media platforms. For instance, if a social media platform does not provide detailed demographic information, some third-party tools might use algorithms to guess this data. These estimates can be helpful but should be taken with a grain of salt. They are often based on generalized data patterns and may not accurately reflect your specific audience. Therefore, it is crucial to use these tools as a supplementary resource rather than relying on them exclusively for critical decisions.

Furthermore, many insights provided by these tools can often be deduced on your own without the need for additional expenses. For example, if you notice that posts made at 9 AM Eastern Standard Time consistently underperform, you might infer that a significant portion of your audience is on the West Coast and still sleeping at that time. By understanding your audience's behavior and preferences, you can make informed decisions about your content strategy without relying heavily on paid analytics tools.

Understanding Time and Audience Reaction

One of the critical aspects of monitoring performance is understanding how the timing of your posts affects audience engagement. Each social media platform has peak times when users are most active. By posting during these times, you can maximize the visibility and engagement of your content.

- Facebook: Generally, the best times to post are between 1 PM to 3 PM during weekdays, with Wednesday at 1 PM and Friday at 11 AM being peak times.

- Instagram: The highest engagement times are typically during lunchtime (11 AM to 1 PM) and evenings (7 PM to 9 PM), especially on Wednesdays and Fridays.

- Twitter/X: Posting between 9 AM to 11 AM on weekdays tends to yield the best results, with Wednesday and Thursday mornings being particularly effective.

- LinkedIn: Since it is a professional network, the best times are during business hours, typically between 10 AM to 12 PM on Tuesdays, Wednesdays, and Thursdays.

- TikTok: The most effective times vary, but generally, early mornings (6 AM to 10 AM) and evenings (7 PM to 11 PM) on weekdays tend to see high engagement.

Pay attention to how your audience reacts to posts made at different times. Use analytics to track engagement metrics for posts published at various times of the day and week. Look for patterns in the data to determine the optimal times to post for your specific audience.

Additionally, consider experimenting with different posting schedules to see how your audience responds. You might find that your particular audience is more active during non-traditional hours or on weekends. By testing different times and analyzing the results, you can fine-tune your posting schedule to maximize engagement.

Adapting Based on Feedback

Feedback from your audience is invaluable for refining your social media strategy. Pay attention to comments, messages, and reviews to gauge how your audience is responding to your content. This feedback can provide insights into what your audience likes, dislikes, and wants to see more of. Actively engaging with your audience and asking for their opinions can also generate useful feedback.

One way to gather feedback is through surveys and polls. These tools allow you to ask your audience directly about their preferences and experiences. For example, you might create a poll asking your followers what type of content they prefer, or a survey to gather more detailed feedback on their needs and interests. Use this information to tailor your content to better meet the expectations of your audience.

Adapting based on feedback also involves making adjustments to your content strategy as needed. If your audience indicates that they prefer more behind-the-scenes content, consider incorporating more of these posts into your schedule. If they express interest in a particular topic, create more content around that subject. By being responsive to your audience's feedback, you can keep your content relevant and engaging.

Implementing changes based on performance analysis and audience feedback is crucial for continuous improvement. For example, if you notice that posts with infographics receive more engagement, consider creating more infographic-based content. If feedback indicates that your audience wants more educational content, focus on producing more tutorials and how-to guides. This iterative process of analyzing performance, gathering feedback, and making adjustments will help you refine your strategy over time.

The Importance of Continuous Improvement

In the dynamic world of social media, staying stagnant is not an option. To remain relevant and effective, you must commit to continuous improvement. This means regularly reviewing your strategy, experimenting with new approaches, and learning from your successes and failures.

One way to foster continuous improvement is by setting regular checkpoints to review your performance. For example, you might conduct a monthly analysis of your social media metrics to assess your progress toward your goals. Use these reviews to identify areas for improvement and set new objectives for the coming month. This process ensures that you are consistently moving forward and making progress.

Experimentation is also a key component of continuous improvement. Don't be afraid to try new content formats, posting schedules, or engagement tactics. Test different approaches to see what resonates with your audience. For example, you might experiment with live video sessions, interactive polls, or user-generated content campaigns. Track the results of these experiments to determine what works best for your audience and incorporate those insights into your strategy.

Learning from both successes and failures is essential for growth. Celebrate your successes and analyze what made them successful so you can replicate those strategies in the future. At the same time, don't shy away from examining your failures.

Understanding why certain posts or campaigns didn't perform well can provide valuable lessons that help you avoid similar pitfalls in the future.

Do Not Overreact to Short-Term Results

It's important to remember that social media success doesn't happen overnight. It's easy to get discouraged by short-term fluctuations in performance, but it's crucial to take a long-term view. Consistency matters more than content for many social media platforms. Algorithms often prioritize consistent posting over occasional viral hits.

There will be times when certain posts won't perform as well as others, and that's okay. It's part of the learning process. Avoid making drastic changes based on one or two underperforming posts. Instead, look for patterns over a more extended period. If a particular type of content consistently underperforms, it might be time to reconsider your approach. However, if it's an isolated incident, it might just be a case of bad timing or other factors beyond your control.

Social media platforms are also motivated to push users toward purchasing ads, sometimes by burying organic posts. While investing in ads can be part of a robust social media strategy, it's essential not to rely on them exclusively. Focus on building a strong organic presence that can support and amplify your paid efforts. Remember that paid ads should complement your organic strategy, not replace it.

Using Advanced Analytics and Tools

To gain deeper insights into your social media performance, consider using advanced analytics tools. Platforms like

Sprout Social, Hootsuite, and Buffer offer comprehensive analytics that go beyond the basics provided by social media platforms. These tools can provide more detailed reports on audience demographics, engagement trends, and content performance.

Advanced analytics tools can also help you track your competitors and understand how your performance stacks up against others in your industry. By analyzing your competitors' strategies, you can identify opportunities to differentiate yourself and capitalize on gaps in the market.

Using these tools, you can also set up automated reports to receive regular updates on your performance metrics. This can save time and ensure that you are always informed about your social media performance. Automated reports can highlight key trends and areas for improvement, helping you make data-driven decisions more efficiently.

However, it is crucial to remember that many of these third-party applications estimate analytics data that isn't directly available from social media platforms. For instance, if a social media platform does not provide detailed demographic information, some third-party tools might use algorithms to guess this data. These estimates can be helpful but should be taken with a grain of salt. They are often based on generalized data patterns and may not accurately reflect your specific audience. Therefore, it is crucial to use these tools as a supplementary resource rather than relying on them exclusively for critical decisions.

Furthermore, many insights provided by these tools can often be deduced on your own without the need for additional expenses. For example, if you notice that posts made at 9 AM Eastern Standard Time consistently underperform, you might infer that a significant portion of your audience is on the West Coast and still sleeping at that time. By understanding your audience's behavior and preferences, you can make informed decisions about your content strategy without relying heavily on paid analytics tools.

In conclusion, analyzing and adapting your social media strategy is essential for long-term success. By regularly monitoring your performance, gathering feedback, and making data-driven adjustments, you can continuously improve your approach and stay ahead of the competition. The next chapter will explore the importance of overcoming challenges and maintaining a healthy balance to ensure sustainable social media success.

Chapter 10: Overcoming Challenges

Navigating the world of social media can be a daunting task, filled with various challenges that can affect your performance and overall well-being. This chapter will explore strategies for dealing with negative feedback, avoiding burnout, and maintaining a positive online presence. Overcoming these challenges is essential for long-term success and sustainability in social media marketing.

Dealing with Negative Feedback

Negative feedback is an inevitable part of being active on social media. No matter how carefully you curate your content or how positively you engage with your audience, there will always be critics. Learning to handle negative feedback constructively is crucial for maintaining your mental health and your brand's reputation.

The first step in dealing with negative feedback is to remain calm and not take it personally. It's natural to feel defensive or upset when someone criticizes your work, but reacting impulsively can escalate the situation. Take a moment to breathe and approach the feedback with a clear mind. Remember, negative feedback can sometimes offer valuable insights that can help you improve.

When responding to negative comments, be professional and respectful. Acknowledge the feedback, apologize if necessary, and offer a solution or explanation. For example, if a customer complains about a product, apologize for their experience and offer to resolve the issue privately. This approach shows that you value your audience's opinions and are committed to addressing their concerns. Publicly handling negative feedback in a mature and constructive manner can also demonstrate your professionalism to other followers.

It's important to differentiate between constructive criticism and trolling. Constructive criticism provides specific feedback that can help you improve, while trolling is intended to provoke and upset. Engage with constructive criticism, but do not feed the trolls. Ignoring or calmly deflecting malicious comments is often the best course of action. For example, if someone leaves a vague or overly hostile comment, you might respond with a simple, "Thank you for your feedback," without engaging further.

Encouraging positive engagement from your loyal followers can also help mitigate negative feedback. When you cultivate a community of supporters, they can often drown out the negativity with their positive interactions. Highlighting user-generated content, positive testimonials, and success stories can reinforce the positive aspects of your brand and create a more balanced view for new visitors.

Finally, use negative feedback as a learning opportunity. Analyze recurring themes or issues mentioned by your audience and take proactive steps to address them. For instance, if multiple customers mention difficulties with your website navigation, consider conducting a usability review and making improvements. By addressing legitimate concerns, you can enhance your products or services and build a stronger, more loyal customer base.

Avoiding Burnout

Maintaining a consistent and engaging social media presence requires significant time and effort. It's easy to become overwhelmed and experience burnout, especially if you're managing multiple platforms or creating content frequently. Recognizing the signs of burnout and implementing strategies to avoid it is essential for your well-being and the sustainability of your social media efforts.

Burnout can manifest as physical and emotional exhaustion, decreased motivation, and a sense of detachment from your work. If you find yourself dreading tasks that you once enjoyed, struggling to maintain focus, or feeling constantly tired, you may be experiencing burnout. Acknowledging these signs early can help you take corrective actions before the burnout becomes severe.

One effective strategy to avoid burnout is to create a content calendar. Planning your content in advance allows you to manage your time more efficiently and ensures a steady flow of posts without last-minute stress. A content calendar helps you organize your ideas, schedule posts, and maintain consistency across all platforms. It also gives you a clear overview of your content strategy, making it easier to balance different types of posts and themes.

Delegating tasks can also help prevent burnout. If you have the resources, consider hiring a social media manager, virtual assistant, or content creator to share the workload. Delegating tasks like scheduling posts, responding to comments, or creating graphics can free up your time to focus on strategic planning and other high-priority activities. If hiring help isn't an option, consider using automation tools to streamline repetitive tasks.

Taking regular breaks and setting boundaries is crucial for maintaining a healthy work-life balance. Designate specific times for social media activities and stick to them. Avoid checking your social media accounts outside of these hours to prevent feeling constantly "on." Incorporate regular breaks throughout your day to recharge and prevent mental fatigue. For instance, you might implement the Pomodoro Technique, where you work for 25 minutes and then take a 5-minute break.

Engaging in activities that promote relaxation and well-being can also help combat burnout. Exercise, hobbies, spending time with loved ones, and practicing mindfulness or meditation can all contribute to your overall mental health. Finding activities that help you unwind and recharge will make it easier to return to your social media tasks with renewed energy and focus.

Finally, regularly evaluate your social media goals and expectations. It's easy to become overwhelmed when you set unrealistic goals or try to do too much at once. Break down your objectives into manageable steps and celebrate small victories along the way. Adjust your strategy as needed to ensure it remains sustainable and aligned with your overall well-being.

Maintaining a Positive Online Presence

A positive online presence is essential for building a loyal following and fostering a supportive community. Your attitude and behavior online can significantly impact how your audience perceives your brand. This section will provide strategies for maintaining a positive and engaging online presence.

Consistency in your tone and messaging is crucial for building trust with your audience. Ensure that your brand voice is friendly, approachable, and professional across all interactions. Whether you're posting content, responding to comments, or handling customer inquiries, maintaining a consistent tone helps reinforce your brand identity and makes your communications more recognizable.

Engage with your audience in a meaningful way. Respond to comments, answer questions, and show appreciation for their support. Personalized interactions, such as addressing followers by their names or acknowledging their specific concerns, can create a more genuine connection. Engaging with your audience not only builds relationships but also encourages more interaction, which can boost your visibility and reach on social media platforms.

Creating and sharing positive content is another effective way to maintain a positive online presence. Highlight success stories, share uplifting messages, and celebrate milestones with your audience. Content that inspires, educates, or entertains can create a positive association with your brand and encourage followers to engage with and share your posts.

It's also important to be transparent and authentic in your communications. Admit mistakes when they happen, and take responsibility for addressing any issues. Authenticity builds trust and credibility, which are essential for long-term success on social media. For example, if there is a delay in product shipping, openly communicate the reasons to your customers and provide updates on the resolution. This level of transparency can turn a potentially negative situation into an opportunity to demonstrate your commitment to customer satisfaction.

Monitoring your brand's online reputation is crucial for maintaining a positive presence. Regularly check mentions of your brand on social media, review sites, and other online platforms. Address negative feedback promptly and professionally, and take proactive steps to resolve any issues. By staying aware of what people are saying about your brand, you can manage your reputation more effectively and respond to potential problems before they escalate.

Being active on social media doesn't necessarily mean constantly coming up with new content to post. It can also mean engaging with other users' posts. Commenting on other posts within your industry or community can help you gain visibility and attract potential followers. Authentic interactions on others' content can show your expertise, build relationships, and increase your chances of being followed by users who find your comments valuable. For instance, if you are a fitness expert, leaving insightful comments on popular fitness influencers' posts can draw their audience's attention to your profile.

Utilizing Support Systems and Networks

Building a supportive network of peers and mentors can provide valuable assistance and encouragement. Join professional groups or communities related to your industry where you can share experiences, seek advice, and gain insights from others who understand the challenges of managing a social media presence.

Networking with other professionals can also lead to collaborative opportunities that enhance your social media strategy. Partnering with influencers, participating in guest posting, or engaging in cross-promotions can expand your reach and introduce your brand to new audiences. Collaborative efforts can also provide fresh perspectives and ideas that reinvigorate your content strategy.

Seeking mentorship from experienced professionals can provide guidance and support as you navigate the complexities of social media marketing. A mentor can offer insights based on their own experiences, help you avoid common pitfalls, and provide encouragement during challenging times. Building relationships with mentors can also open doors to new opportunities and resources that aid your social media journey.

Balancing Authenticity and Professionalism

Balancing authenticity and professionalism is key to maintaining a positive online presence. While it's important to be genuine and relatable, it's also essential to uphold a level of professionalism that reflects well on your brand.

Authenticity involves being true to your brand's values and personality. Share behind-the-scenes content, personal stories, and insights that humanize your brand and make it relatable. However, ensure that your content aligns with your brand's image and maintains a level of professionalism. For example, while sharing a personal story about your business journey can be engaging, avoid sharing overly personal or controversial content that could alienate your audience.

Professionalism involves maintaining a respectful and courteous demeanor in all interactions. Avoid engaging in arguments or responding negatively to criticism. Instead, approach every interaction with a calm and constructive attitude. Professionalism also extends to the quality of your content—ensure that your posts are well-crafted, free of errors, and visually appealing.

In conclusion, overcoming challenges in social media requires a combination of strategic planning, emotional resilience, and continuous learning. By effectively managing negative feedback, avoiding burnout, maintaining a positive online presence, utilizing support systems, and balancing authenticity with professionalism, you can navigate the complexities of social media marketing and achieve long-term success. The next chapter will delve into case studies and success stories, providing practical examples of how these strategies have been applied effectively in real-world scenarios.

Chapter 11: Case Studies and Success Stories

Learning from the experiences of successful brands and individuals can provide valuable insights into effective social media strategies. This chapter will explore several case studies and success stories, highlighting the approaches and tactics that have led to their success. By examining these real-world examples, you can gain practical ideas and inspiration for your own social media efforts.

Sweetgreen – Growing a Restaurant's Following Through Social Media

Sweetgreen, a fast-casual restaurant chain known for its healthy salads and grain bowls, has effectively used social media to grow its following and build a strong brand presence. Sweetgreen's success can be attributed to its strategic use of visual content, community engagement, and brand storytelling.

Sweetgreen's social media strategy focuses heavily on high-quality visuals. The brand regularly posts mouth-watering photos of its dishes, highlighting the freshness and quality of its ingredients. These visually appealing posts not only attract food lovers but also reinforce Sweetgreen's commitment to healthy eating. The use of professional photography and vibrant colors makes their posts stand out in users' feeds, enticing followers to engage with the content.

Community engagement is another cornerstone of Sweetgreen's social media strategy. The brand frequently interacts with its followers by responding to comments, reposting user-generated content, and running contests and giveaways. For example, Sweetgreen might ask followers to share photos of their favorite salad combinations using a branded hashtag. This not only generates user-generated content but also creates a sense of community among its customers. Engaging with followers in a genuine and personal manner helps build loyalty and encourages word-of-mouth promotion.

Brand storytelling is also central to Sweetgreen's social media success. The company shares stories about its sourcing practices, partnerships with local farmers, and sustainability efforts. By highlighting the ethical and environmental aspects of their business, Sweetgreen connects with customers who value transparency and social responsibility. These stories not only enhance the brand's image but also build a deeper emotional connection with its audience.

Sweetgreen's case study demonstrates how restaurants and food brands can leverage social media to grow their following and build a strong brand presence. By focusing on high-quality visuals, community engagement, and authentic storytelling, Sweetgreen has successfully created a loyal and engaged online community.

Neil Patel – Building Authority Through Valuable Content

Neil Patel, a renowned digital marketing expert, has built a massive following by consistently sharing valuable and actionable content. Patel's journey in digital marketing started with a genuine desire to help businesses grow by understanding the intricacies of online marketing. He began by sharing detailed, actionable insights through his blog, focusing on topics such as SEO, content marketing, and social media strategies.

Patel's blog posts are often comprehensive guides that break down complex concepts into manageable steps, making it easier for readers to implement his advice. By consistently providing high-quality content, Neil has built a reputation for being a reliable source of information in the digital marketing industry. His willingness to share his expertise and insights freely has not only built his brand but also attracted numerous clients who seek his professional services.

In addition to his blog, Neil uses other mediums such as YouTube videos, podcasts, and social media posts to share his knowledge. His transparency and willingness to share valuable insights have earned him a large following across multiple platforms. This multi-channel approach not only broadens his reach but also reinforces his expertise. By giving away substantial value for free, Neil has demonstrated the principle of reciprocity. His audience feels a sense of gratitude and trust, which translates into loyalty and a preference for his services when they need professional digital marketing assistance.

Patel's success illustrates the importance of providing value and building trust through transparency and consistency. By sharing detailed, practical content that addresses the needs of his audience, he has established himself as a thought leader in digital marketing. His case study demonstrates how focusing on delivering value can lead to long-term success and a loyal following.

Dr. Sandra Lee (Dr. Pimple Popper) – Engaging Content and Community Building

Dr. Sandra Lee, also known as Dr. Pimple Popper, gained widespread recognition by sharing educational and entertaining content about skincare and dermatology on social media and YouTube. Dr. Lee's approach to content creation involves a mix of educational posts, entertaining videos, and personal interactions. She often shares detailed explanations of various skin conditions, treatments, and preventive measures. Her videos, which show her performing procedures, are not only informative but also satisfy a certain curiosity that many viewers have.

Dr. Lee's transparency and willingness to share her expertise have built a large, loyal following. People appreciate her approachable manner and in-depth knowledge, which has led to a significant increase in her clinic's visibility and patient base. Moreover, Dr. Lee frequently engages with her audience through Q&A sessions, live videos, and social media comments. This direct interaction helps her build a personal connection with her followers, making them feel valued and heard.

By consistently providing valuable content and engaging with her audience, Dr. Lee has effectively utilized the principle of reciprocity. Her followers feel a sense of gratitude and trust, which has translated into increased business for her clinic. The success of Dr. Lee's online presence highlights the importance of combining valuable content with genuine engagement to build a loyal and trusting audience.

Dr. Lee's case study emphasizes the power of combining education with entertainment to create engaging content. Her willingness to share her expertise and interact with her audience has built a strong community around her brand. This case study demonstrates how building a personal connection with your audience can lead to increased loyalty and business growth.

Gary Vaynerchuk – Leveraging Authenticity and Multichannel Presence

Gary Vaynerchuk, a serial entrepreneur and social media personality, has built a massive following by being authentic and leveraging a multichannel presence. Gary started by documenting his business journey and sharing his insights on entrepreneurship, marketing, and social media. His content is characterized by its raw and unfiltered nature, which resonates with many people.

Vaynerchuk's approach involves being present on multiple platforms, including YouTube, Instagram, LinkedIn, and Twitter. He tailors his content to fit the unique characteristics and audience of each platform. For example, he uses Instagram for motivational posts and behind-the-scenes content, while LinkedIn is more focused on professional advice and business insights.

Gary's authenticity and transparency have built a strong personal brand. He openly shares his successes and failures, making his content relatable and trustworthy. This honesty has fostered a loyal community that actively engages with his content and supports his ventures. By consistently providing value and maintaining a genuine connection with his audience, Gary has become a leading voice in the business and marketing world.

Gary Vaynerchuk's success underscores the importance of authenticity and adaptability in social media marketing. His ability to connect with his audience on a personal level and tailor his content for different platforms has been key to his growth. This case study highlights how being genuine and versatile can enhance your social media strategy and build a dedicated following.

Marie Forleo – Creating a Supportive Community

Marie Forleo, a life coach and motivational speaker, has successfully built a supportive community through her online content and programs. Marie started by sharing her insights on personal development, business, and life coaching through her blog and YouTube channel. Her content is designed to inspire and empower her audience to pursue their goals and overcome challenges.

Forleo's approach involves creating content that is both educational and motivational. She shares practical advice on business and personal growth, often featuring interviews with successful entrepreneurs and thought leaders. Marie's content is characterized by its positive and uplifting tone, which resonates with her audience.

Marie Forleo has also built a strong community around her brand through her online programs, such as B-School, an online business training program for entrepreneurs. By offering valuable resources and fostering a sense of community, Marie has created a loyal following that actively engages with her content and participates in her programs.

Marie's success highlights the importance of creating a supportive and empowering community. By providing valuable content and fostering a positive environment, she has built a dedicated audience that trusts and supports her. This case study demonstrates how focusing on community building and providing value can lead to long-term success.

Warby Parker – Growing a Retail Store's Following

Warby Parker, an eyewear retailer, has effectively used social media to build a strong brand presence and engage with its audience. The company's success on social media can be attributed to its innovative marketing strategies, community engagement, and authentic storytelling.

Warby Parker's social media strategy includes a mix of high-quality visuals, user-generated content, and interactive campaigns. The brand regularly posts photos and videos showcasing its stylish eyewear, customer experiences, and behind-the-scenes content from their design and production processes. These posts highlight the quality and craftsmanship of their products, making them more appealing to potential customers.

User-generated content plays a significant role in Warby Parker's social media strategy. The company encourages customers to share photos of themselves wearing Warby Parker glasses using branded hashtags. By reposting these photos, Warby Parker not only showcases its products but also builds a sense of community among its customers. This strategy helps foster brand loyalty and encourages word-of-mouth promotion.

Interactive campaigns are another key component of Warby Parker's social media strategy. The company often runs contests, polls, and Q&A sessions to engage with its audience and gather feedback. For example, Warby Parker might ask followers to vote on their favorite frame styles or participate in a photo contest. These interactive elements create a dynamic and engaging social media presence, making followers feel more connected to the brand.

Warby Parker also leverages storytelling to connect with its audience on a deeper level. The company shares stories about its founding, mission, and commitment to social responsibility. By highlighting their efforts to provide affordable eyewear and give back to communities in need, Warby

Parker creates a positive brand image that resonates with socially-conscious consumers.

Warby Parker's case study demonstrates how retail brands can effectively use social media to grow their

following and build a strong brand presence. By focusing on high-quality visuals, community engagement, and authentic storytelling, Warby Parker has successfully created a loyal and engaged online community.

Conclusion

These case studies illustrate various strategies for achieving success on social media. From providing valuable content and engaging with your audience to leveraging authenticity and building a supportive community, each example offers practical insights that you can apply to your own social media efforts. By learning from the experiences of successful individuals and brands, you can develop effective strategies that resonate with your audience and drive long-term success.

Understanding what to expect next is crucial in the world of social media. Just as listeners tend to favor songs that feel familiar, your audience will respond positively to consistent and predictable content. Consistency in the types of posts you share is essential for building trust and familiarity with your audience. Too many people make the mistake of trying to directly monetize their following too soon, which can alienate their audience.

For instance, allowing for ads as a way to make money can hurt the following you are building. Imagine if any of the examples in this chapter had inserted ads in the middle of their growth phases. It would have made them look inauthentic and caused followers to question the authenticity of every subsequent post. Instead, focus on providing consistent, valuable content that reinforces your brand's identity and message.

Consistency also means avoiding the temptation to post the same content across all platforms. Tailoring your content to fit the unique characteristics of each platform ensures that your audience has a reason to follow you on multiple channels without feeling like they're seeing the same thing everywhere.

By applying these principles, you can build a loyal and engaged audience that values your content and trusts your brand. The next chapter will explore future trends in social media, providing insights into emerging platforms and technologies that will shape the social media landscape in the coming years. This forward-looking approach will help you stay ahead of the curve and adapt your strategy to leverage new opportunities.

Chapter 12: Future Trends in Social Media

The landscape of social media is constantly evolving, with new platforms, technologies, and trends emerging regularly. To stay competitive and relevant, it's crucial to stay informed about these changes and be prepared to adapt your strategies accordingly. This chapter will explore the future trends in social media, providing insights into emerging platforms and technologies that will shape the social media landscape in the coming years.

Emerging Platforms and Technologies

While established platforms like Facebook, Instagram, and Twitter remain dominant, new social media platforms are continuously emerging, offering unique features and opportunities for users and marketers. Keeping an eye on these platforms can help you identify new opportunities to reach and engage with your audience. One such platform is Clubhouse, an audio-based social network that gained popularity for its live, interactive discussions and networking opportunities. Clubhouse allows users to join virtual rooms and participate in conversations on various topics, making it an excellent platform for thought leaders and brands looking to host live events and engage with their audience in real-time.

Another platform to watch is TikTok, which, although not entirely new, has continued to grow exponentially, becoming one of the most influential platforms, particularly among younger audiences. Its short-form video content and algorithm-driven feed provide unique opportunities for viral marketing and creative content. Additionally, Meta's Threads app is designed for close friends, allowing users to share status updates, photos, and messages with a select group, emphasizing privacy and intimacy. This makes it a valuable tool for building tight-knit communities. Snapchat, despite being a well-established platform, continues to innovate with features like augmented reality (AR) lenses and interactive content. Brands can leverage Snapchat's unique features to create engaging and immersive experiences for their audience.

Augmented Reality (AR) and Virtual Reality (VR) technologies are becoming increasingly integrated into social media platforms, offering new ways to create immersive and interactive content. Brands can use AR to create engaging filters and experiences, while VR can be used for virtual events and product demonstrations. AR filters, popularized by platforms like Instagram and Snapchat, allow users to overlay digital effects onto their photos and videos. Brands can create custom AR filters to promote their products and engage with their audience in a fun and interactive way. Virtual reality offers new possibilities for immersive content, allowing brands to host virtual events, product launches, and interactive experiences in a virtual environment. As VR technology becomes more accessible, it's likely to become a more significant part of social media marketing strategies.

Artificial Intelligence (AI) and machine learning are revolutionizing social media by providing advanced analytics, content recommendations, and automated interactions. These technologies can help brands better understand their audience, optimize their content, and improve engagement. AI-powered analytics can analyze vast amounts of data to provide insights into audience behavior, preferences, and trends. This information can help brands tailor their content and strategies to better meet the needs of their audience. AI-powered chatbots can automate customer service interactions, providing instant responses to common queries and freeing up time for social media managers to focus on more complex tasks. Chatbots can also engage with users in real-time, offering personalized recommendations and support. Additionally, machine learning algorithms can analyze user behavior and preferences to recommend content that is likely to be of interest, helping brands increase engagement by ensuring their content reaches the right audience at the right time.

Future Trends and Innovations

Social commerce, the integration of e-commerce features into social media platforms, is set to grow significantly. Platforms like Instagram and Facebook have already introduced shopping features that allow users to purchase products directly from posts and stories. This trend is expected to continue, with more platforms incorporating e-commerce capabilities. Shoppable posts enable brands to tag products in their posts, making it easy for users to click through and purchase items without leaving the platform. This seamless shopping experience can drive sales and increase conversion rates. Live shopping, which combines live streaming with e-commerce, is becoming increasingly popular. Brands can host live shopping events where they showcase products and interact with viewers in real-time, creating a sense of urgency and excitement that encourages viewers to make purchases during the live event.

Video content continues to dominate social media, with platforms like YouTube, TikTok, and Instagram leading the way. Short-form videos, live streaming, and interactive video content are particularly popular, offering engaging ways to connect with audiences. Platforms like TikTok and Instagram Reels have popularized short-form video content, which is ideal for capturing attention quickly and conveying messages succinctly. Brands can use short-form videos for product demos, tutorials, and behind-the-scenes content. Live streaming allows brands to connect with their audience in real-time, offering opportunities for Q&A sessions, product launches, and virtual events. Live video content is highly engaging and can help build a sense of community and authenticity.

As concerns about privacy and data security continue to grow, social media platforms are taking steps to protect user data and provide more transparency. Brands must prioritize data security and ensure they comply with privacy regulations to build trust with their audience. Social media platforms are implementing features that give users more control over their data and how it's used. Brands should be transparent about their data collection practices and provide clear information on how user data is used and protected. Adhering to privacy regulations like the General Data Protection Regulation (GDPR) and the California Consumer Privacy Act (CCPA) is essential for maintaining trust and avoiding legal issues. Brands should stay informed about changes in privacy laws and ensure their practices are compliant.

The rise of niche communities and micro-influencers is a significant trend in social media. Users are increasingly seeking out smaller, more focused communities where they can connect with like-minded individuals. Micro-influencers, who have smaller but highly engaged followings, are becoming valuable partners for brands. Brands can engage with niche communities by participating in relevant groups, forums, and discussions, connecting with highly engaged audiences interested in specific topics or products. Partnering with micro-influencers can be more cost-effective and impactful than working with larger influencers. Micro-influencers have a strong connection with their followers and can provide authentic recommendations that resonate with their audience.

Joining new social media platforms as soon as they emerge is crucial for securing your brand's username. Having the same username across multiple platforms helps maintain a consistent brand identity and makes it easier for your audience to find and recognize you. When a new platform gains popularity, early adoption increases the odds of obtaining your preferred username before someone else does. This proactive approach ensures that your brand remains cohesive and professional across all digital channels.

Staying Ahead of the Curve

Staying ahead of the curve in social media requires continuous learning and adaptation. Experimenting with new content formats and features can help you discover what resonates with your audience. Keep an eye on emerging trends and technologies in the social media landscape by following industry blogs, attending conferences, and participating in online communities. Regularly interacting with your audience to gather feedback and insights can help you tailor your content and strategies to better meet their expectations. Investing in continuous learning by taking online courses, attending workshops, and reading industry publications can expand your knowledge and skills.

Conclusion

As we look to the future, it's clear that the social media landscape will continue to evolve, driven by new platforms, technologies, and user behaviors. By staying informed about these trends and being willing to adapt, you can position your brand for long-term success.

Understanding what to expect next is crucial in the world of social media. Just as listeners tend to favor songs that feel familiar, your audience will respond positively to consistent and predictable content. Consistency in the types of posts you share is essential for building trust and familiarity with your audience. Too many people make the mistake of trying to directly monetize their following too soon, which can alienate their audience. For instance, allowing for ads as a way to make money can hurt the following you are building. Imagine if any of the examples in this chapter had inserted ads in the middle of their growth phases. It would have made them appear inauthentic and caused followers to question the authenticity of every subsequent post. Instead, focus on providing consistent, valuable content that reinforces your brand's identity and message.

Consistency also means avoiding the temptation to post the same content across all platforms. Tailoring your content to fit the unique characteristics of each platform ensures that your audience has a reason to follow you on multiple channels without feeling like they're seeing the same thing everywhere.

By applying these principles, you can build a loyal and engaged audience that values your content and trusts your brand. The next chapter will explore future trends in social media, providing insights into emerging platforms and technologies that will shape the social media landscape in the coming years. This forward-looking approach will help you stay ahead of the curve and adapt your strategy to leverage new opportunities.

Chapter 13: Conclusion

As we conclude this journey through the intricate world of social media, it's important to reflect on the key insights and strategies we've explored. The landscape of social media is dynamic and ever-changing, but the principles and psychological concepts that underpin successful engagement remain consistent. By understanding and applying these principles, you can build a strong, authentic presence that resonates with your audience and drives meaningful interactions.

Recap of Key Points

Throughout this book, we've covered a wide range of topics designed to help you navigate the complexities of social media. We started with an overview of social media's influence, emphasizing the importance of cultivating a genuine and engaging presence. We discussed the psychological underpinnings of online behavior, including cognitive biases, the role of dopamine in social media usage, and the impact of FOMO.

Building a solid foundation is crucial, and we've detailed how to choose the right type of content for each platform, create a consistent brand identity, and understand your audience. Content that captivates is at the heart of social media success, and we've explored various types of engaging content, from high-quality visuals to compelling written content and interactive formats.

Storytelling emerged as a powerful tool for building connections and trust with your audience. By leveraging psychological principles like reciprocity, social proof, scarcity, and urgency, you can create content that not only engages but also converts. Building a community and fostering engagement is essential, and we've provided strategies for creating a sense of belonging, engaging with your audience, and collaborating with other profiles.

Maximizing your reach requires an understanding of social media algorithms, the importance of early interaction, and platform-specific insights. We've also highlighted the significance of combining blogs with social media for maximum impact, emphasizing the value of educational content in building trust.

Analyzing and adapting your strategy is a continuous process. Monitoring your performance, adapting based on feedback, and avoiding overreaction are key to staying relevant and effective. Overcoming challenges such as negative feedback and avoiding burnout are critical for long-term success.

The case studies and success stories of individuals and brands like Sweetgreen, Neil Patel, Dr. Sandra Lee, Gary Vaynerchuk, Marie Forleo, and Warby Parker provide real-world examples of how these principles can be applied to achieve remarkable results.

Words of Wisdom

As you embark on your social media journey, it's important to remember that what works for one person or brand may not necessarily work for you. Authenticity is key. Be true to yourself and your brand, and let your unique voice shine through in your content. The principles outlined in this book can be applied to various types of content, whether it's videos of you speaking, still images, or any other format that suits your style and message.

One of the most effective ways to establish yourself as a thought leader in your field is by sharing valuable information. Many people hesitate to share their knowledge, fearing that it will reduce the demand for their services. However, the opposite is often true. When you share your expertise freely, you demonstrate your depth of knowledge and establish yourself as an authority in your field. This transparency builds trust with your audience, who will come to see you as a reliable source of information.

Consider the example of an attorney who shares insights into the music industry or a mechanic who explains the causes of common car noises. By offering this valuable information, they help their audience understand complex issues, which in turn builds trust and positions them as experts. This strategy not only attracts potential clients but also fosters a loyal following that values and respects their expertise.

Consistency is crucial. Just as listeners prefer songs that feel familiar, your audience will appreciate consistent and predictable content. Avoid the temptation to directly monetize your following too soon. Focus on building trust and providing value before considering monetization strategies. Allowing for ads can undermine the authenticity of your content, making your audience question the sincerity of your posts.

It's also essential to adapt and stay informed about emerging trends and platforms. Joining new platforms early to secure your username and experimenting with new content formats can give you a competitive edge. Engage with your audience regularly to gather feedback and refine your strategies based on their preferences.

The Importance of Sharing Knowledge

Sharing knowledge is a cornerstone of establishing yourself as a thought leader. When you provide valuable insights and information, you show your audience that you are knowledgeable and willing to help. This approach can significantly enhance your credibility and authority in your field.

For instance, if you are a digital marketer, sharing detailed guides on SEO best practices or social media strategies can demonstrate your expertise. If you are a fitness coach, posting videos explaining the correct form for exercises or offering nutritional advice can help your audience see the value in your content. By doing so, you not only educate your audience but also build a strong foundation of trust.

Trust is a fundamental element in any relationship, including the relationship between you and your audience. When people trust you, they are more likely to engage with your content, recommend you to others, and ultimately become loyal followers or clients. Sharing your knowledge openly and generously can accelerate this trust-building process.

Furthermore, sharing valuable content can lead to increased engagement and interaction on your social media platforms. When you provide content that genuinely helps your audience, they are more likely to comment, share, and like your posts. This increased engagement can boost your visibility and reach on social media, as platforms often prioritize content that generates a lot of interaction.

Final Thoughts

The journey of building and maintaining a social media following is ongoing. It requires dedication, creativity, and a willingness to adapt to changing trends and technologies. By applying the psychological principles and strategies outlined in this book, you can create a social media presence that not only engages but also drives meaningful interactions and growth.

Stay curious, stay authentic, and most importantly, stay committed to providing value to your audience. Social media offers immense opportunities for connection, growth, and success. Embrace these opportunities with an open mind and a strategic approach, and you'll be well on your way to achieving social media success.

Remember, social media is not just about posting content; it's about building relationships and creating a community. Interact with your audience authentically, and show genuine interest in their feedback and concerns. By doing so, you can foster loyalty and trust, which are the foundation of a strong social media presence.

Appendix

Additional Resources

For further reading on social media marketing and psychology, consider exploring the following books, articles, and websites:

- "Influence: The Psychology of Persuasion" by Robert B. Cialdini

- "Made to Stick: Why Some Ideas Survive and Others Die" by Chip Heath and Dan Heath

- "Contagious: How to Build Word of Mouth in the Digital Age" by Jonah Berger

- Social Media Examiner (www.socialmediaexaminer.com)

- HubSpot Blog (blog.hubspot.com)

Tools and Platforms

A list of recommended tools for social media management, analytics, and content creation:

- Hootsuite: A social media management platform that allows you to schedule posts, track performance, and engage with your audience.

- Buffer: A social media scheduling tool that helps you plan and publish content across multiple platforms.

- Canva: A graphic design tool that simplifies the process of creating visually appealing social media graphics.

- Google Analytics: A web analytics service that tracks and reports website traffic, providing insights into your audience and their behavior.

- Sprout Social: A social media management and analytics platform that offers tools for scheduling, monitoring, and analyzing your social media performance.

With these resources and tools at your disposal, you're well-equipped to navigate the ever-changing world of social media and build a successful online presence. Embrace the journey, stay informed, and always strive to provide value to your audience. Your social media success story is just beginning.